SMALL LIBRARIES
second edition

SMALL LIBRARIES

A Handbook for Successful Management

SECOND EDITION

by Sally Gardner Reed

McFarland & Company, Inc., Publishers
Jefferson, North Carolina, and London

Library of Congress Cataloguing-in-Publication Data

Reed, Sally Gardner, 1953–
Small libraries : a handbook for successful management /
by Sally Gardner Reed.—2nd ed.
p.   cm.
Includes bibliographical references and index.
ISBN 0-7864-1238-0 (softcover : 50# alkaline paper) ∞
1. Small libraries—Administration—Handbooks, manuals, etc.   I. Title.
Z675.S57 R44 2002   025.1'974—dc21   2002004602

British Library cataloguing data are available

On the cover—background photograph: New London Public Library,
New London, Ohio *(Mary Ellen Armentrout)*;
foreground photography by Marty McGee.

Manufactured in the United States of America

*McFarland & Company, Inc., Publishers
Box 611, Jefferson, North Carolina 28640
www.mcfarlandpub.com*

In memory of my mother,
Sara Jane Gardner
1933–1993

and in honor of Dudley Colbert, Olivia Osei-Sarfo,
Sherry Clem, Peg Hagel and Bettie Goganious,
who for many years have run small libraries in Norfolk, Virginia—
often against all odds but always with a singular dedication
to improving the lives of those in their communities

and for Yvonne Hilliard-Bradley of the Norfolk Public Library,
who for nearly 30 years has pulled it all together

Contents

Introduction

When I wrote the first edition of *Small Libraries* about ten years ago, I worked and lived in a small town in Vermont. At that time a group of entrepreneurial librarians came up with this marketing slogan: "Libraries—Keepers of Tradition, Catalysts for Change." So much has changed since then, and surprisingly, so much is still the same. Perhaps the slogan was prophetic, or perhaps it was simply reflective of the role libraries have always played.

So, what has changed? For one thing, I've moved on from Vermont and the small library I ran in Middlebury. Until recently I worked and lived in Norfolk, Virginia, having spent a few intervening years in Ames, Iowa. Rather than directing a small library, I ran a metropolitan library system (albeit a relatively small one by large library standards). The Norfolk Public Library is comprised of a central library, 11 branches, a homework center, and a bookmobile. So how can I possibly retain credibility to offer you this updated version of *Small Libraries*? It's pretty simple, actually—everything I knew about running the Norfolk Public Library I learned from my experience in running small libraries.

It's true. Working in small libraries teaches you everything you need to know—from ordering, cataloging, and covering books; to working with and getting the most from your staff; to knowing exactly how to make one dollar stretch to buy $1.35 worth of service! I am absolutely convinced that I became a much better director because I began my career running small libraries and I understood both the challenges and the joys of delivering services to a small, intimate community that the staff has come to know on a personal basis. In fact, large library systems are really just collections of small libraries banded together under one administration. We know in large systems just as in small libraries that the smaller you are, the closer you get to the community you serve. And as in small towns and communities across America, branch libraries in cities are the center of the neighborhoods they serve. It was heartening for me to know that in many ways, I never left small libraries—I just had more of them!

The changes that have been most stunning for me and certainly for us all have to do with the explosion of information technology and what that means for the delivery of services. Who knew ten short years ago that we would be investing as much in our technological infrastructure as many of us do in books? Could we have imagined the incredible opportunity of the Internet and the infinite universe of information and possibility it brings to even the smallest hamlet of America? Could we have foreseen a time when we could offer the same online access that is offered at the New York Public Library? In our wildest marketing dreams, did we conceive of a service so popular that we would hardly be able to keep up with patron traffic? I remember when I thought I was staying "in front of the curve" because I remembered to request plenty of electrical outlets in a library's new addition! And finally, who would have thought that libraries would some day be facing federal mandates to filter information or be accused of not caring about children?

This second edition has been updated to address many of the concerns and issues that are presented with the new technology. Technology has gained more than a foothold; it is now so pervasive and so integrated in our lives that it's often hard to keep perspective on technology as a tool rather than an end in itself. We are often asked if libraries will even be necessary in the 21st century given the advent and growth of the Internet. Just when we thought the Information Age would finally give the community information center (read: library) the political clout we've long fought to obtain, we are actually being challenged to prove our future relevance. This, of course, normally comes from local leaders and nonlibrary users—the rest of us know that computers and Internet access have brought unprecedented numbers of new users into the library. Talk about relevance!

It is clear that technology has had a profound effect on services in even the smallest of libraries. Certainly, the changes in information retrieval and reference are the most obvious. No longer is it enough for us to have a good handle on the traditional print publishing scene. If we wanted to change our image of being "bookish," it looks like our wish is coming true. Though books are still at the heart of our services (and may it ever be thus!), we now must continue to educate ourselves in a rapidly changing digital environment. It is critical that those running small libraries learn about information technology and how to use it to serve our patrons.

Even though technology has forced us to be far more aggressive in our continuing education, it has offered us an opportunity to bring our patrons together with the information they need as never before. In some ways, our roles have changed from being information providers to being "information guides and mentors." Our expertise in knowing how to sort through the chaff to come up with the exact information that suits each individual's unique needs is expertise we now share with our patrons so that they can become more effective navigators through the vast and growing Internet.

Though libraries have always been a civic investment in literacy in its broadest sense, we are coming to understand more than ever that because technology is penetrating all aspects of life, our new century requires everyone to be a lifelong learner. The change we experience in our libraries is replicated in everyone's lives. The library has a critical role to play in providing learning opportunities of all types for all people. Because we know that, despite our best efforts, not everyone uses the library, more emphasis must be given to aggressive outreach services. If we are going to be a useful resource for those who need intellectual enrichment, we are going to have to find those who might be left behind and reach out to them. This edition reflects a greater emphasis on outreach. To paraphrase legendary hockey player Wayne Gretzky, we need to skate to where the puck is!

Despite the limitless possibilities, advances in information technology have also brought with them some enormous challenges. Because the entire spectrum of information is available, we are faced with the fact that not all information on the Internet is what we would choose for our patrons, especially our children. Many if not most of us would agree that there is information on the Internet that is not what we'd select for our libraries in our former environment where space and funding were natural limiting agents. How can a small library that benefits so dramatically from a technology that provides a universe of information ward off charges that libraries are, therefore, no longer safe places for children? As I write this edition, libraries are faced with increasing legislative efforts to require filtering software for public computers. At this time, we know that filtering software is far from perfect and that these technological solutions filter out much of the good along with the "bad." In addition, we know that filtering software can "leak," allowing those images that it was designed to keep out of view to come through.

In this edition, I address this issue, and I encourage librarians and library staff to continue to do what they have always done for children: Guide them in the use of the library's resources. The Internet affords us an unprecedented opportunity to help children become critical thinkers and good consumers of this new digital technology that is their future. Each library will make decisions in the coming years about how to balance the "miracle" of information that is the Internet with the concern for children and what children see when they come into the library. Philosophically it is important, I believe, to hold high the bar for intellectual freedom, and I am convinced that librarians across the country will weather this storm and find ways to continue to provide the greatest access possible to the greatest number of people.

This brings me around to what has not changed. The most heartening part of updating this book was in finding through the rereading how much our core values and our worth to our communities have remained the same. Libraries are as critical as ever to the intellectual well being of the community. Literacy, in its broadest sense, is more important to individual success than ever before. Now our citizens must be able to read *and* have at least rudimentary technological skills as well if they are to succeed in life. Our world is being automated at an astounding rate, and jobs that once required nothing more than manual labor are increasingly being redesigned to take advantage of automation for inventory, process improvement, and front-line management of tasks. Libraries have traditionally been the place where people from all walks of life and with all kinds of needs have found assistance and support for lifelong learning. That hasn't changed. What has changed are the formats and tools we are using to deliver information and, as discussed earlier, the new and enormous access to information we have online.

Libraries today are still important civic spaces where people come to learn and share in a variety of ways. In fact, it could well be argued that libraries *as places* are more important than ever before. Perhaps the real threat in the information age isn't that libraries will no longer be needed, but that people will lose more and more opportunities to gather and interact as a result of remote access to banking, shopping, entertainment, and yes, even learning. There must be an intuitive understanding about the importance of libraries as "place" because at this writing, library building is currently undergoing a renaissance around the country. What is interesting about the new library buildings is that they are being built with a greater recognition of the need for public meeting rooms. We are, after all, social beings, and libraries have always been a place for people to come together and share ideas and information, and to learn from one another. Libraries are continuing to fill that need.

While it is true that online resources have replaced to some degree the numbers and types of print resources we need, the fact is that we are still mostly about books. At this point in time, at least, most of our space is occupied by bookshelves. Children still check out armloads of picture books, best-seller waiting lists are still a mile long, and although you can use the Internet to get almost any information on the history of, say, Virginia, our patrons are still turning to our book collections to get that history of Virginia. Collection development (of the tangible sort) is still at the heart of what we do. Sure, the formats are constantly changing: Long gone are the LPs, and even cassettes are an endangered species; here today are CDs, and even these are soon to be replaced by DVDs. Who knows what's next! Whatever it is, I am confident that we will find ways to ensure that we can provide it. It's challenging all right, but it's nothing new.

The importance of hiring and nurturing an excellent staff is still critically important and again, perhaps even more important than ever. Library staff must have every opportunity to learn and grow with our changing environment. If libraries are becoming more important as social and civic places, library staff must continue to see excellence in public service as the number-one priority. We can retain and develop our staffs only by respecting them and giving them the guidance and authority they need to make good decisions in the workplace and to deliver high quality services.

In addition to paid staff, libraries still rely—as well they should—on the services of volunteers. Bringing volunteers into the library and nurturing them is not only still a good way to enhance service delivery, it is also an excellent way to build community and develop committed and knowledgeable advocates.

Which brings me to something else that hasn't changed: the need to continually make the case for your library. I am sorry to report that in the last ten years, despite the fact that libraries have been early and successful adopters of technology for the community, despite the fact that more people walk through our doors with a greater diversity of need than ever before, we are still typically underfunded. Someday I might be able to revise this book without a chapter on developing a political base, but that day has not yet arrived.

In my opinion those who are running small libraries in the 21st century are both pioneers and heroes. Although our commitment to service and to ensuring access to information for all people is central to what we do, we are also working harder than ever before to ensure that libraries stay at the heart of the community. Small libraries continue striving to offer the full range of services that their larger counterparts do, but they do it with smaller staffs, fewer dollars, less specialized expertise, and often with less political clout. They do it with heart.

Most libraries in America could be classified as "small" libraries. That's great—because I know that small is beautiful!

ONE

Creating a Political Base

As we move increasingly into a world where borders are no longer barriers—literacy, education and access to information become more and more important to all our citizens. In truth, our democracy depends on it. Now that technology has upped the "information ante" those who do not have access to information technology, and who do not have the know-how they need to make sense of it, need libraries. In rural and small-town America, the public library is very likely the only place where both information technology and the staff to help citizens use it well are available to everyone—for free. Wow! It's truly an amazing concept and one that, for all the high-tech glitz, is the very same concept upon which the public library was founded. Now, we must resell this important concept to those who fund us.

Directors of small libraries have always been advocates—for their library's services, budget, and place in the community. They know, however, that even though their library is heavily used and ranks high in patron satisfaction, those who fund libraries all too often see our services as peripheral—nice but not really critical. Certainly, library budgets, as small as they are, can be cut or level funded without too much damage. Now, more than ever, we must help our town leaders understand where the damage lies when the library is not properly funded and supported.

It is sadly ironic that while libraries are becoming more important than ever before in the Information Age, many of those who shape our fate believe the exact opposite. What librarian today has not been asked why libraries matter anymore now that we have the Internet? Not only is the demand for library services growing and becoming more complex, the battle for funding is, all too often, becoming more difficult. And it's not just about the operating budget. Without educating our communities and especially our community leaders about the importance of the library in the future, getting funds and support for bricks and mortar can be tricky indeed.

Being effective political advocates is just part of the job these days—if we don't engage in this effort and do it well, it's possible that someday we'll have nothing left to advocate. The future of library services depends on us. Advocacy is education—not just about the services we offer but why those services are critical to our communities. We must ensure that those who fund us understand well that burgeoning information technology is not making the library less important but more so. In addition, we must be honest about the growing costs of providing adequate service. It's not as though traditional formats (books, magazines, audiovisual materials) are being replaced by online technology, instead our services are enhanced by it. We need both. Sure, we can be excellent financial resource managers and ensure that we do not duplicate resources in various formats unless patron demand dictates. Some of the magazines we subscribe to for research purposes may be included in online packages but again, if we subscribe to periodical databases we are really enhancing the information and material available to our patrons, and not, in large part, replacing print. This is a good thing. We shouldn't apologize about the costs but celebrate the ability we have, even in the smallest community, to provide our patrons with rich and abundant resources never before possible. Yes, there is a cost but our job is to help our funders understand that the cost is very low compared to the value of this service and compared to the costs of ignorance.

The "we can't afford it" attitude becomes a self-fulfilling prophecy, when applied to adequate salaries, pay for staff to attend conferences, meaningful collection development, or hours that truly serve the needs of your patrons. No library can operate successfully and be a dynamic part of the community fabric without adequate resources. Unless your library is heavily endowed or you have a town that has more public money than it can spend, you will have to be an outspoken advocate for your library and learn to compete effectively for limited funds.

It is probably true that most of us who run small libraries have reasons that are somewhat similar for our choosing librarianship as a profession. It wouldn't be surprising to find that most of us were seduced into the field by a love of books and people and the opportunity to work with both. I'm not so sure that many of us would say a love of the political arena and advocacy brought us to the field, and in a way, that's too bad.

Like it or not, you will probably find that behind every successful library there is a librarian who knows how to get what he or she needs. Getting what you need means knowing who to approach and how to approach them. A good librarian must be able to motivate and persuade trustees, friends, town management, local businesses and all the people in the community.

Even if you feel satisfied that the level of funding you receive each year is all that you need and want, it would be shortsighted to think that you will never need the political consensus to be on your side. If you are well funded, then you probably have a very satisfied patronage. A satisfied patronage tends to burgeon as your success in meeting demand generates even more demand from current patrons. Also, the word-of-mouth grapevine will spread the good news about your library bringing in new patrons.

Even if the economic climate in your town never changes, we know that opportunities to bring information and learning resources to all your patrons are growing and changing almost daily. In addition, the day may come when you need to add more space, significantly change the library's environment to accommodate changing technology, or drastically increase the development of a particular collection. In short, the time may come when you need really big bucks to accomplish a new goal.

If you have a satisfied and loyal clientele, your battle is half won. You must, however, convince your board of trustees that your new needs are worth fighting for. (If your library has never done battle for the budget itself, the idea of doing so now for the sake of new goals will probably not be enthusiastically embraced by the board at first.) You must also be prepared to convince the town government (few of whom, typically, use the library) that your goals are both valid and worthy of a major capital outlay. You must, in short, become a political activist.

Whether we think of ourselves as activists or not, most of us get experience with the political powers-that-be each year when we must explain once again why the library is worth spending money on. Whether you are fighting for more staff hours, higher salaries, better benefits, improved collections or more space, you will find that you will have to be a skillful politician to get the money the library needs.

Trustees as Advocates

What terrific potential we have in our trustees, yet frequently talk among librarians about trustees is fraught with anger and frustration. It appears from casual observation that trustees may be the biggest stumbling blocks to success in many small libraries. At least it is true that many librarians perceive this to be the case.

Too often, trustees of small public libraries tend to adhere to the "don't rock the boat" mentality. This is really no great surprise. Consider the average board of trustees of a small-town library: typically, library lovers who are elected or appointed to terms of various lengths. It is the exceptional case where there is a job description for trustees, where experience is required, or where knowledge of the library profession is a prerequisite.

Do the trustees understand that implicit in their role is the need to go to bat for the library when it has been established by them and the director that salaries are too low, that benefits are unfair (especially when compared to fellow town employees), and that space limitations are interfering with the ability to provide good or even adequate service? These are important issues and must be addressed by the trustees even when it means confrontation with town officials or the requirement to face the public to press the point home.

Trustees don't often get into the library act with the understanding that their role might well require political activism any more than many of *us* did. That is why as library director, it is crucial for you to raise the political consciousness of the members of your board. If you cannot create a "political base" with your trustees, the game is lost. You will be forever convincing the board, on the one hand, that salaries are too low, and on the other hand failing to persuade them to publicly fight for higher salaries. I think trustees often feel they are doing the admirable thing by keeping the spending in check and keeping the library out of the political limelight.

Saying that trustees must be motivated to become library advocates in the political arena is easy; accomplishing that goal is another matter altogether. If you don't work hard on making it happen, however, you are shirking a good portion of your responsibility. You as director are responsible for the health and vitality of the library. If you set goals and then fail to do what is necessary to accomplish them (e.g., get the resources and political support you need), you are not doing your duty. Similarly, if you are ignoring avenues for growth and service because getting the money to accomplish them will be "impossible," you are again shirking your responsibility.

So, how do you create a politically active and vocal board? The first step is fact gathering. Look at your library objectively. Sit down with your staff and create the ideal situation—throw in everything you want regardless of cost. Brainstorm and fantasize. After you feel you have the perfect library for all time, go back to the drawing board and put the dreams into perspective, but don't link any of your plans to money or the lack thereof. Once you have created a library that is responsive to your community and its needs, both articulated and perceived, figure out how much money it would take to turn your library into that place. Don't forget extra staff hours, publicity and printing costs, added materials costs, and perhaps even added facilities costs such as fuel, electricity or phone.

Take this plan to the trustees. Open discussion. Find out if your ideal is supported by them. See if you can get them, while discussing this ideal, to forget for the moment how much it would cost. If you have fundamental disagreements with the trustees about where the library should be heading and what kinds of service it should be providing, reveal these disagreements. Ask them if they would be interested in surveying the public about services to see if there is a desire out there for you to do more. Be sure to encourage their involvement in the formulation of the survey if they agree to support one. You don't want your findings disputed because the trustees feel the public was led to give the answers you were looking for.

If the trustees refuse to continue the dialogue and exploration, if you cannot garner any support *and* you have no hope that the current complexion of the board is likely to change in the near future, you may have arrived at a true impasse. One reasonable but seldom recommended suggestion is: quit. If you can take this route (be on the lookout for openings in nearby towns before you make the move or consider similar types of jobs, as a bookstore manager, for example), it might be your best solution. Of course, many of us are tied to our community because of family or other important considerations, so simply moving away to take another job is not in the cards. If you are bound to the area and feel this is the job that makes sense for you, you will have to come to terms with the situation, making whatever improvements are possible within the boundaries in place. In the meantime you can look for the possibility that a real live wire will join the board and pitch the battle for or with you even if you have to recruit that potential trustee yourself.

If, on the other hand, the board is willing to discuss growth and even agrees that the goals you have set are good and reasonable, congratulations—you have reached first base (in the first inning). Now is the time to toss in what is often perceived to be the foul ball—the cost according to your best estimates. You have a subtle edge if you have gotten the trustees to agree to your goals. If they then balk solely on the basis of "lack of funding," there is the strong implication that they are ignoring their responsibility as trustees by dismissing good and meaningful plans out of hand before they even try to get the money necessary to accomplish them.

You may, of course, have to point this out to them—and you should. The trick is to do so very tactfully. Suggest that all of you (include yourself here) need to pursue avenues of funding or you will be turning your backs on providing the service you feel you should be providing. Just be sure in doing so you leave their integrity and self-respect intact. If you get the trustees on the defensive you will accomplish nothing; that's what being a good politician is all about.

Be ready now to suggest ways to get some of the funding you need. Look at your list of goals; work together with the trustees to prioritize them. If you feel the number-one problem facing your library right now is low salaries, then present ideas to them for solving that problem and that problem only, for now. Trying to tackle the whole list of goals at once will be overwhelming for all of you, especially if you are new to this world of activism. Additionally, your real-world chances of getting everything you want right now are slim indeed.

You may decide, in the issue of salaries, that once you begin your campaign you are going to adhere to your bottom-line requests (these should be based on reality and your "don't rock the boat" trustees will probably ensure this). What you may be willing to compromise on, however, is the phase-in period. It may be decided that salaries need to be increased 20 percent to put them on a par with similar jobs in your town but you are willing to accept a 10 percent increase this year with the promise of another 10 percent next year.

Winning this first battle may not be easy, but there are ways to put the weight on your side; these (involving Friends of the Library, influential members of the community, and patrons) will be discussed below. Nevertheless, if you have persuaded the trustees to actively enter this battle with you, you have made the first step in creating a political base. If you are successful—and there is every likelihood you will be if you lay the groundwork properly—your trustees may become a little heady and insist that you now look at the second priority on your list.

Long term you do have the ability to shape the culture of your board. In addition to bringing them into the planning and budget discussions and getting them on board with your goals, you can and should develop and orientation for new board members that makes it clear that advocacy is part of their jobs. Contact your state library and see if they have materials that you can give new trustees outlining expectations of trustees beyond rubber stamping and chair warming. Take a new trustee to lunch and talk about your goals and aspirations for library service. Let her know how she can help. Just as with our employees, the best chance we have to shape commitment and outline our expectations for performance is in the very beginning. If your board of trustees have a "hands off" attitude and history when it comes to political action, be sure you get to a new trustee first with your enthusiasm and firm belief that he or she is just the person you need to really make a difference.

You Gotta Have Friends

Friends of the Library are utterly indispensable to the highly successful community library. Traditionally, they are known for holding fabulous book sales and spending all that glorious money on you, but they are worth so much more to you than the money they bring in. They are a built-in lobbying group.

Because the best gift the Friends can give you is the gift of political support, you may want to consider a proposal to your Friends group (if you have one) or to a "start up" committee (if you don't)—that membership to the Friends group begin at a low $1.00 per year. It's true that membership dues often constitute a significant portion of the group's revenues. It's worth considering, however, a basic membership of $1.00 with encouraged categories, for example, of "sponsor" for $10.00, "patron" for $25.00 or "saint" for $50.00

The most successful Friends group I know has this arrangement. The vast majority of members select a category of $10.00 or more but others, with less money to spare, are not left out. What this group has in the end is a coffer full of money from membership dues *and* an extremely large support group that can be counted on to get to the polls or call their town officials when the library needs their support.

STARTING A NEW FRIENDS GROUP

If you don't already have a Friends group, don't procrastinate! You *need* a Friends group. It might not be easy to get a group together, but it can be done and it will pay off for years to come.

Discuss with your trustees the benefits of this group; cite other libraries in your area that have benefited. If you have a trustee who is especially interested or committed to the idea, you might be able to turn the enterprise of forming such a group over to him. Be sure that you are involved in the follow-up, however.

The formulation of any support group rarely happens without a good deal of initial enthusiasm by some one person—and in the end that person is likely to be you. After discussing the idea with your trustees (and getting the approval to go ahead) you should contact several of your patrons or volunteers who might be persuaded to join the group. If you can enlist the help of, say, five dependable people, you can become a committee with the purpose of establishing a Friends group.

Because you want your Friends group to be politically powerful, you should work hard to get a community leader or several if possible, involved in the formative stages. Think about who holds has power in your town. In every community there are those who influence the decision-makers. It might be the spouse of the mayor; it might be the owner of a key business; it might be a former and well-respected member of your town's council—perhaps a former mayor. Try to appeal to the politically connected in your town on the basis of their knowledge of the town and their expertise in getting things done. Even if you have to ask them to participate for just the initial stages of the Friends' evolution, you will likely find that this person develops a sense of ownership if they decide to get involved. Chances are that any VIP you are able to recruit will stay involved; but even if that doesn't happen, you will have created a new and powerful ally in the process.

The start-up committee should initially focus on two things. The first is to establish purpose and get 501(c)(3) status as a non-profit organization. The second is to generate participation and support. The statement of purpose (see Appendix A—Friends of the Library "Statement of Purpose") should be developed with input from you, the committee and the trustees, and should fall within the guidelines of general library policy. You should also participate in meetings to keep the group aware of priorities for spending and keep the group in touch with library goals so they can be effective advocates on your behalf.

Once you have established the guidelines for operation, you need to spread the word. Let your community know what you're up to and why you need this support group. Be sure your publicity includes contributions made by other Friends groups in the area and includes, as well, the fun things they do both to raise money and to generate interest in the library. Once the word is out, begin to plan your first exciting meeting of the Friends of the Library.

The first meeting should be as carefully planned as any major program your library sponsors. It should be exciting enough to draw a wide (and hopefully) diverse group of people. You might convince a local "celebrity" to give a talk for free as a gift to the library and to help you get the group off the ground. Following whatever wonderful program you plan, have one of the committee members preside over a short business meeting. This meeting should include a reading of the statement of purpose, and a plea should be made for more members to join the committee. The most important thing about this first meeting is that it be enthusiastic and successful. Good roots are needed for the long-term health of the group.

Have another committee meeting within the month and be sure to personally invite all those who expressed interest. It may take some real work on your part to keep the group motivated but if you plan another program for the following month, you will find that your committee will continue to grow. After about six months' time (when you've met with the group at least four times) you should have a core of people who can look at that statement of purpose and begin to think of ways to raise money and support for the library.

MAKING AN EXISTING FRIENDS GROUP MORE EFFECTIVE

You are very fortunate if you already have a Friends group. Of course, your notion of "helping" and theirs may be quite different, and it's important to get your goals aligned before waging any political campaigns dependent (at least in part) on their support.

If your existing Friends group does not have a written statement of purpose you should all work on one before going any further. Because the Friends exist to support the library, it makes sense that the library (that is, the trustees and the director) participate with the Friends in drafting this statement. I know of one case (and it may be typical) where the Friends have existed so long in such an autonomous state that their assistance to the library has become almost counterproductive.

The problem at the "Mudville Public Library" is that over the past several decades the Friends group has functioned without strong involvement from the library director or any member of the library staff. Without guidance, they have set their own agenda for spending. If they perceive a need for a new set of encyclopedias, that's what they buy. If they think the children's room needs a new table and chair, they order them. These gifts (well intended, to be sure) are then ceremoniously handed over to the Mudville librarian who is expected to use them as the Friends planned and to assume a grateful posture. In addition, being advocates for public support for the library never even occurred to the Mudville Friends.

Several librarians have come and gone and not one was able to muster the courage to approach the Friends with a prioritized list of needs. These librarians felt that any such move would be perceived as turf encroachment at best, ingratitude at worst. Unless you are willing to share the responsibilities of collection development and facilities planning and maintenance with your Friends, as became the case in the Mudville scenario, it is important that you work with this group in defining their role and yours.

The best way to incorporate the Friends into the library fabric in a meaningful way is to invite the Friends' president to attend and participate in a special trustee meeting where you discuss goals and objectives. At this meeting, you will be explicit as to where you see the Friends (and their gifts and their political support) fitting into this picture. Since working well with Friends is a two way street, be sure that the Friends representative has a chance to share the vision that the Friends have for the library and how they view their role with regard to support. Together, you can develop mutual goals and expectations. Have the board ask the president to address these goals with the Friends group at their next meeting and ask them to work with you in drafting a Statement of Purpose for their group. (See Appendix A—Statement of Purpose.) If a member of your board can be persuaded to attend the next Friends meeting you will have established a good first step in developing a better partnership between the library staff, the trustees and the Friends.

All this sounds pretty straightforward and simple but when a history of autonomy has developed for any group, you are likely to encounter some resistance and hurt feelings in your program of change. The implication will be that you wish to take away a degree of their previous autonomy and they may infer from that (rightly perhaps) that you were not satisfied with their prior assistance. Remember how important this group is to your library and use all due tact, never ceasing to show your respect and appreciation. The bottom line remains, however, that the Friends must operate within the framework that you and the board have adopted.

MAKING THE MOST OF YOUR FRIENDS

Once you have the Friends working *with you* in the fullest sense, you will have a group at your disposal worth more than any new set of encyclopedias or fabulous new piece of furniture. This is a group that has already shown their support by giving time and money to you; it's only a short step from here to political support if you need them.

If your library is dependent on town support for its health, you will need to convince the taxpayers that it is worthy of their expenditures. It may be possible for you and the board to win the vote every time, but your best insurance policy is to have a vocal group that is representative of your community and is clearly not acting out of self-interest.

As you set goals and objectives with your Friends, be sure that library advocacy makes it to the top of the list.

Establishing Clout with the Town Government

It is absolutely critical to your library's success that you establish yourself as a dynamic, credible, and key leader in your community. Though you are at an advantage in having a constituency to help you make the case for your library (see "Co-opting Community Support" below), the quickest and most direct way to get the support you need is to have significant clout yourself. This is no easy task. The reality is that due to the less than powerful image that continues to linger around librarianship, the strides you make in gaining personal power in your community will likely come from the dint of your own personality and commitment to being an articulate and outspoken advocate for libraries.

Luckily there are ways that even a rookie politico can begin to be seen as a leader within the government structure. To begin with, you should establish yourself as an expert in the evolving information infrastructure. Take and make opportunities to talk about the importance of a literate and technologically literate citizenry to your town's well-being. Stay up to date on policy issues that will affect your patrons and your town's residents and keep your town manager and fellow department heads up to date. It is important for them to see you as the intelligent, thoughtful team member that you are.

In addition to becoming more outspoken about the ways in which the library can contribute to a "smarter" community, be seen as a leader in other areas of town governance as well. As important as it is to keep the library's message alive, it is also important that you are seen by your town manager and by town council members as a "can do" person who is interested in the welfare of every aspect of town services. Step up to the plate. Volunteer for committee appointments that have nothing to do with library services. Consider participation in a civic organization as well. The Rotary Club or a well-known and respected charitable organization such as the United Way are also vehicles to gain personal visibility and respect. Be seen as a team player and problem-solver in a variety of venues. When you do participate in finding ways to accomplish other town goals, be active. Speak up. Contribute intelligently and positively to the team. When you establish yourself as someone who clearly has the best overall interests of your town at heart, you will have a much more receptive audience when you get back to library issues.

This is important. Lack of power and prestige with town governments has to rank right near the top of the list of reasons small public libraries offer inadequate salaries and unsatisfactory or no benefits, operate on a "shoestring," and encounter resistance when they need to expand or rebuild. If the people making the spending decisions have a low regard for the value of libraries and you as the librarian, you will have a difficult job in convincing them to raise their level of financial support in any significant way.

Looking at it from the town official's point of view, the existing level of support given by the town to the library makes sense. In all probability, if you haven't established yourself as a community leader with the credentials that your city leaders honor and respect, your singular protestations on behalf of the library and its budget will be easy to ignore as the predictable whining from the usual suspect.

The power you gain (or fail to gain) as librarian will impact the regard town leaders have for library services themselves. We know this. The most deadly threat you'll want to recognize and deal with is that ever-popular statement made by local government officials right before they cut your request for funding. The statement usually starts with something like this, "We'd really like to help the library out; it's not as though we're against you. After all, libraries rank right up there with apple pie and motherhood…" When was the last time you heard a similar kiss-of-death platitude applied to roads, police protection, civil rights or education? When your town officials begin to respond to your request with this all-too-common sentiment, you can be sure the big "but" is right on its heels. Apple pie is fattening and we all know what kind of respect motherhood commands in our society. What this kind of statement does is make officials seem supportive. The key word here is "seem." Don't expect anyone with this sort of condescending attitude to put any money where her mouth is.

Financial Support

THE LOFTY ARGUMENT

Let's get this mom and apple pie stuff out of the way from the beginning. Libraries have their own unique value and it's value worth paying for. Town governments must be continually reminded that citizens both need and are entitled to information—information that would be unobtainable (either because it is literally unavailable or because it is too expensive) if it weren't provided by libraries. As technology works to continually change information delivery modes and increase the amount of information available, the library and the librarian become even more critical to the notion of access.

No one really likes to prioritize the importance of a library's various services. In fact, to do so can seemingly discriminate against user groups who are in the minority. If, for example, we say that children's services are most important, we are also saying (at least by implication) that service to adult new readers is less so. It's a corner most of us would really not like to be backed into. Our various services meet a diversity of needs and we (typically) judge all needs to be basically equal.

I have to say, however, that I do feel our information services are our most valuable commodity, especially so in a political sense. Looking closely at the role and justification for public libraries in our society today, I see information access becoming more and more important, as the means of getting information and the nature of information itself become more and more complex. Information is power and libraries can and should play a role as the great equalizer among the information haves and have-nots.

Thomas Jefferson once said, "If a society expects to be civilized and free in a state of ignorance, it expects what never was and never will be." Perhaps this eloquent statement epitomizes best what is at the heart of library philosophy. Libraries are important because they provide a necessary bridge for the gap between ignorance and a well-informed society. Freedom of the press is probably one of our most cherished and closely guarded rights because freedom of the press translates into our right to know. Oppression by governments is dependent on an ignorant and ill-informed people. The press, however, in all its forms (newspapers, magazines, television, radio) is necessarily confined by space and time in what information it can provide. Not only that, but it is unrealistic to believe that the choices necessitated by space and time do not reflect bias—we are influenced by what the press *chooses* to print, show or tell.

Public libraries are committed to making sure that patrons have access to an almost unlimited amount of information. Clearly advances in computerized information retrieval are now transcending spatial constraints and are allowing libraries to fulfill their roles as information providers regardless of space limitations. The barrier to access faced by the public now is cost. Public libraries have existed on a share-the-cost model from the beginning. In recognition that much of the information available out there would be unobtainable to the average person, money is pooled and the costs and resources are shared to support a common library. This is what taxation is all about and this is the message that must be continually delivered to those who hold the purse strings. It is no easy task to convince a political body that it is their responsibility as public servants to help protect the citizens' right to know. It is, however, a compelling argument and one we need to voice again and again.

Because this right to know is so fundamental, in hard times I believe it will become our *raison d'être*. It will be easy for town governments to argue that schools provide educational and leisure reading for children and that the provision of best sellers and videos is a luxury. It would be much more difficult for any government body in our country to argue that citizens should have less access to knowledge and information.

I would never argue that our services to children, the elderly and the homebound, or programs and best sellers, are invalid or even unimportant. In fact, lifelong learning and literacy are, themselves, access issues. Nevertheless, our chief mission is to ensure that access to the broadest possible scope of information is available to our citizenry without barriers. I firmly believe that our democracy depends on it.

THE ARGUMENT FOR IMMEDIATE NEED

While it's true that you want to present and reiterate the basic importance of libraries to your town government whenever the opportunity arises, it is also true that you have more practical needs that must be addressed now. Whether you wish to enhance patron access to online resources, raise salaries, increase space, improve collections or simply keep your budget from being cut, you will have to work at proving that your request is reasonable and valid.

The groundwork has been laid if you have established yourself as a community leader and information expert, if the trustees have been actively working on your behalf, and if the Friends are aware of and in agreement with your stated needs. Your town officials are elected and they do care what the general public thinks. It's up to you to be sure they know that you have support for your request from the citizens in your town.

Before you approach the people in your town who make the budgetary decisions, be sure you've done your homework. The very first thing to ensure is that your trustees have agreed to go all the way in your attempt to get the funding you request. Help them out by gathering all the facts necessary to support your case and making a fact sheet (fairly well detailed) available to them.

If you are going for better salaries, for example, be sure to include average salaries for similar library positions in your area, your state and nationwide. If your state association has established a minimum entry-level salary recommendation, be sure all the trustees know what it is. Also find out what other town employees are making (the salary range for their positions is public information) and get copies of their position descriptions. Make objective comparisons for education, skill and job requirements and present these comparisons in a clear, concise way. Whatever the need (even if it's a battle to avoid a cut), document your request with facts and figures.

If you are attempting to negotiate a major increase in your budget, or you have reason to believe that without a good fight your budget will be cut, you will probably do well to bring in the Friends of the Library. Once you have the trustees well-informed and motivated on the library's behalf, make a formal presentation to your Friends group. This presentation will serve two functions. First, it will give you practice before a friendly audience (be sure to encourage questions and criticisms; you will get plenty of these from the town government). Second, you need to enlist the Friends' *active* support. Once you've made your presentation and answered all their concerns and questions, let them know that you will need help in convincing the town government that your request is important and worth funding.

If you can get your Friends group to help, they might very well make the difference between success and failure. You and the trustees will be perceived by the town officials as being self-interested; your "objective" opinion regarding the legitimate need of your request will be tainted by that perception. Your Friends group, however, has nothing to gain but better library services in getting the funding required. Their voices are likely to be regarded as much more representative of those of the public at large.

Given the particular clout that members of your Friends group are likely to have, you should work to organize their efforts. If you are an employee of the town manager and not of the trustees, you may need to let the trustees take the lead in working with the Friends to manage an advocacy effort. Together the trustees and Friends can begin to make the case for better funding for your library, with the Friends being the most visible advocates.

Depending on the resistance you feel you are likely to encounter for your request, Friends can be encouraged to call the officials responsible for the budget and speak on behalf of the library. In addition, Friends can also ask others in the community who use and benefit by library services to make calls as well. Friends and advocates should identify themselves as library supporters and they should have a fact sheet that you have prepared which documents the need for the request and answers anticipated questions.

When the budget hearing is scheduled, ask members of the Friends group to come to voice their support. Again, be sure they are well-informed and, above all, polite and deferential. It might be more than a little intimidating for your town officials when you show up to the hearing with 25 other people. While you do want the added support of your "lobby," you must also do your best not to put the officials on the defensive.

Although bringing in help from your Friends group can be a highly successful strategy, you should use this approach judiciously. The effectiveness of this pressure from a "lobby" is dependent in part on its departure from standard procedure. If you bring in a large support group every time you approach the town budget-makers, they will begin not only to expect it but resent it as well. You do want to show the town that you can stand on your own two feet, but once in a while, when circumstances are special, your approach should be special too.

Year-Round Advocacy

During budget time, we have the opportunity to present the library in its best light and make articulate statements about why the library is important to the community and why it should be supported. To be honest, this is something I love to do. Having this chance to speak publicly about the importance of library services always "reconnects" me with why I got into this profession in the first place. For most of us, library work fills an important need to do something meaningful with our lives. Yet, often in the day-to-day grind to provide the best services possible (often with ridiculously low budgets), we forget that mission mentality that brought us into the field in the first place. Once a year, we get to take center stage in our towns to articulate our passion about libraries.

As articulate and persuasive as you might be at this once-a-year opportunity, however, the effectiveness of this effort will increase immeasurably if you have done a good job in promoting the library throughout the year. Because every town-supported library can be helped or hurt by the town government, it makes sense to do what you can to endear the library to those who make up that government all year long. It takes little time and effort to put members of the select board or town council on a mailing list for the library's newsletter. You might also suggest to the Friends that these people be put on the mailing list for any newsletter your Friends group might publish. If you have an end of the year holiday celebration, why not ask your town officials to attend?

Because it is true that people will give their most unstinting support when there is "something in it for them," you should be sure that your town officials know about the services and materials at the library that will have direct value for them. Find out what their particular interests are and let them know what kinds of materials are available to enhance those interests. Ask them if they would be interested in having a "professional collection" set up at the library with materials on city and town management. Above all, be sure that each town official has a library card!

THE POWER OF THE PRESS

Almost every library publishes a newsletter. If you don't, start now! The power of the press is at your fingertips when you publish a library newsletter. That power, however, is lost or at least extremely limited if you use this newsletter only to tout the wonderful "goings-on" at your library. Sure it's important to be informative but you have an even greater opportunity, if you use your newsletter well, to persuade and educate.

Here's a simple way to turn an OK newsletter into a powerful political tool. With every article you write and every event you promote, ask yourself one simple question before you begin writing: why does this *matter*? I think one of the biggest mistakes librarians make in promoting their libraries is assuming that everyone understands the importance and value of what we do. Certainly those who support us understand that, but to be politically effective, we need to convert the apathetic (read city leaders), not the choir.

When you write an article about an upcoming event, don't just report the who, what, where, and when. Be sure to be very clear about the *why*. In fact, I recommend starting there. For example, if your library is planning to sponsor a program featuring folk dancers, begin your article with a few sentences on how we are becoming a global community and your library is providing a doorway to that world and its many different cultures. Talk about how libraries have always been a path to broadening horizons and how your community benefits by a population that is understanding and sensitive to different cultures. Then you can give the details. Pretty simple, right? If you are listing new acquisitions, take the opportunity to tell why these materials matter to your community (not just users, but the community at large—remember, we're trying to get beyond the choir here!). A listing of new children's books gives a wonderful opportunity to discuss literacy and the importance of early exposure to books. New resume guides or other self-help books give you the opportunity to tout the role your library plays in helping people with transitions in life at all ages.

Once you have designed a newsletter that is politically powerful, interesting (lots of pictures help), and informative, be sure you get as much mileage out of it as you can. Develop a mailing list that includes the town manager and the town council. You may also want to include members of the community who have influence. Mailing the newsletter out each month to supporters or potential supporters is an extremely easy way to keep your library on important community members' radar screens.

Many libraries manage the costs of producing and mailing a newsletter by asking the Friends to sponsor it. The Friends might even be encouraged to contribute an article of their own each month. Many Friends groups tout receiving the newsletter in the mail as an incentive to join. If you do not have a newsletter, talk to your Friends soon about their support for this new venture.

Another effective tool that libraries generally have at their disposal to both inform and promote the library outside the library's walls is the press release. Just a short article written every week or every other week will do a wonderful job in keeping the library in public view.

Hopefully the days are gone of library press releases that simply list, week after week, the new titles at the library. Everyone knows (or nearly everyone) that the library gets new books. Much more interesting are the "book" articles in which you highlight certain topics that the library has materials on. Write an article about your books on parenting, sports, or exercise for example. Give a brief summary of the titles you list and recommend. If you want to push some especially interesting new books, you might include a few quotes from the reviews. Because we've been so successful in getting the word out that we offer books, a more valuable approach in writing press releases might be to promote some of the lesser known functions your library fulfills as a way of promoting it and its importance in the community. Just as with your library newsletter, you want anything you write for the local paper to show clearly why your library's services matter.

Before writing your next press release, think about what (if you could pick only one thing) you would like the town officials and taxpayers to know about your library. Is it the degree of growth your library experienced over the past ten years? Is it the fact that you have fabulous reference services? Would you like them to know that you circulate more children's books per capita than any other public library in the state? Whatever your particular message might be, let that be the centerpiece of your press release.

Let's say you are interested in getting more hours for library service. You know that to be open longer you will need more staff and that means more money. You know it will be a tough battle to convince the town officials, even though the trustees are in complete agreement that the library needs to be open more hours in the week. Start a subtle campaign well before budget time via the press. Be sure that whoever writes your copy is good at it. Your message could well backfire if it shows the public that you can't write or express yourself well. With that in mind, here's an example of the first press release you might publish in your "awareness" campaign:

LIBRARY CIRCULATION TOPS 200,000!

Library Director Sally Reed announced that library circulation topped 200,000 for the first time ever in 2002. "This figure represents an equivalent of 18 items checked out for each man, woman and child living in our town, a value of over $540 if purchased individually," explained Reed. Library circulation has been steadily climbing over the past decade and the 200,000 figure is an increase of 124 percent over circulation in 1989.

"What's really exciting about this number," reports Reed, "is that it means our town is reading and learning every day. It's been predicted that the Internet will make reading and books obsolete; clearly that's not the case here. In a country where illiteracy rates are alarming, it is good to know that in our town, people understand the value of lifelong learning and the importance of the library in supporting that value."

The Smalltown Public Library first opened its doors in 1912. In that year statistics show circulation of library materials to have been 17,434. Reed attributes the dramatic upswing in library usage in recent years to a marked increase in service to children. "Parents seem to be much more aware of the value in reading for children," said Reed. "We often have new parents inquiring about library cards for their infants!"

While the circulation of materials is high in comparison to that of other libraries of similar size in the state, Reed reports that the number of hours the library is open falls short of the average. "We are looking into ways to increase our hours of service to the community," said Reed. "The desire for increased opportunity to use the library seems clear."

The Smalltown Library is open Mondays, Wednesdays and Fridays from 10 to 6, Tuesday and Thursdays from 2 to 8 and Saturdays from 10 to 2. Call 123-4567 for more information.

Every time you write a press release you should ask yourself if you are getting all the mileage you can out of it. If you are announcing a program, throw in the fact that the library sponsors an average of 25 programs a year. If you are promoting your reference services, why not throw in a quote about the importance of information access as we head toward the next century (there are plenty to choose from in any library periodical). The point is, you want all your readers to know not just what you have to offer, but why it is important as well.

LOCAL RADIO AND TELEVISION

If you're lucky, you live in or near a town with a radio station or a local television station. Don't be shy. Contact the managers at these stations and let them know you would welcome the opportunity to promote the library. If something really special is happening at the library, it would make a good icebreaker for the initial contact. In any case, local stations often welcome input from local agencies and organizations.

Once you've grabbed the opportunity to be on the air, you will need to come fully prepared. If you are appearing to pitch a specific event or occasion (National Library Week usually will get you in), your job will be easier. It might be too that you'll get yourself a half hour on the local talk show and be asked to suggest a topic. If this is the case, choose something that has wide interest and that you are very comfortable talking about. The history of your own library *might* be interesting; censorship is usually a hot topic; the impact technology is having on information retrieval and publishing can be interesting, especially if you show how your own library is bringing information technology to your users.

If you are not comfortable speaking in public, appoint someone from your library who is; either a well-spoken staff member or a trustee would be best. Another idea would be to sponsor a short reading each week (about 15 minutes) on the radio where staff members, trustees, and Friends who are good at reading aloud take turns reading from their favorite titles. It would be fun to include some kids in the action too, reading from some of their favorite works. Talk to your local radio station to see if you can sell them on the idea. You might get your foot in the door by asking for this opportunity each day during National Library Week. If you do an out-standing job, you may well convince the station owners that this is an idea that has appeal to the radio audience. Whatever the topic and whoever the speaker, it is crucial that the presentation is intelligent and professional. Remember, your mission is to gather clout as well as to promote the library.

Co-Opting Community Support

Our patrons are our best friends in making the case for our libraries. They are the ones who benefit directly from our services and they are the ones who will come to the library's defense if it's threatened. Our patrons don't need to be told why the library is important, but they do need to be told what they can do to ensure that our library is secure and that it retains a place of importance in the town's budgetary priorities. They also need to know what it takes to provide the services they've come to love and appreciate. Be sure that throughout the year you share with them the various services you perform—both behind the scenes and publicly. Not all patrons use all your services, but they should know the full scope of the services you offer, and they should know why those services matter.

There is probably no better method of establishing the support of the community than to serve them well. Everything you do to understand and meet their needs will serve you in times of hardship. You must remember, however, that it's human nature to take things for granted. Although when asked, most library patrons would attest to their love and support of libraries, the average patron has little idea what it really takes to ensure responsive library service for a wide variety of people.

It is important to make both your efforts and your needs public. Bring the library's light out and let it shine every chance you get!

Two

Personnel—The Library's Most Valuable Asset

It's true—the staff *is* the library's most valuable asset. If you have any doubts, take a look at your budget. In almost all cases, the cost of personnel is the library's largest line item. Even if you have mostly volunteers on your staff, you know how important they are to the quality (or lack thereof) of your service. Given the importance of good library employees, it is easy to understand that one of the director's most important roles is to develop the best staff possible. A good working staff does not just materialize; it is carefully selected and nurtured. In order for you to develop hardworking and enthusiastic library employees, you must provide both encouragement and opportunity for all staff members to grow in their jobs. You must be extremely careful in your hiring practices and continually evaluate performance, offering advice and support for growth and improvement. Even volunteers should be treated professionally as they come on board and throughout their tenure (see "Volunteers" below).

To say that librarians and their staff are the library's most valuable assets isn't a radical notion; but to back up that statement in a tangible way apparently is. It is critical for directors of small libraries everywhere to *do something* about encouraging staff members' professional growth. Here's what I suggest for starters. Get out your library's budget and find the line item that says "Mileage and Conference." Cross it out. Write in "Staff Development."

Now that you've more clearly defined what this line item is really for, see if there is enough money in this category to fully reimburse each staff member for their attending at least one workshop or conference during the course of the year. If there isn't, take enough money from your materials budget to cover what you need in "Staff Development." With just a few strokes of your pencil you have paved the way for your library and its employees to become more productive, more efficient and more committed to providing excellent service than ever before.

Of course taking money out of the book budget is a sacrifice, but as the old adage goes, "first things first." Even though library employees would have a hard time justifying their professional existence without materials to catalog and make available to patrons, without a good staff to select, order, organize and disperse those materials, they're just so many books in the jobber's warehouse.

Now that you've taken the first step to put your money where your values are, you can begin to explore the many different ways to develop an excellent staff. What kind of staff members are you trying to develop? A good staff member understands and shares your vision of library service. This person loves libraries (especially yours) and works hard to promote them. In addition, a valuable staff member has initiative and follow through. One of the easiest and most efficient ways of accomplishing the task of, say, running the children's room of the library is to hire a dynamic children's librarian who only needs to be pointed in the right direction. Once that's done, your involvement with that portion of the library's services is greatly reduced. In fact, if you've done your initial job of hiring well, you need only be on hand to give the children's librarian all the encouragement, advice, and recognition he deserves; then you can sit back and bask in the reflected glory.

Hiring

The opportunity to hire a new staff member is an opportunity to bring fresh ideas, perspectives and commitment to the library. Through it, you can make a major (and possibly long-term) impact on your library and how it functions. Hiring new staff members is one of your most important responsibilities as director. It should never be taken lightly and expedience should not be considered a virtue. Take the time you need to hire just the person you want. In small libraries with small staffs, it's important that you don't delegate this responsibility away—or at least not entirely. You may well have your children's librarian take the lead in hiring an assistant, but you should be sure that your values for hiring only the best are shared and employed.

Because your library is small, everyone working in it has the ability to directly influence the quality of service it delivers. You want a person who will be a productive member of the staff, who will share in developing goals and objectives, and who will play an important and effective role in making the library even better. You want only the best.

So, how do you go about hiring this paragon? Where do you find him, and how do you know you've got the right person when the interviewing is over? A careful, systematic approach will go a long way here.

RECRUITMENT

To get the best possible pool of applicants for any job opening, you will have to be creative and resourceful—not to mention aggressive. Because you want as broad a selection of qualified applicants as possible, consider every means you have at your disposal for creating interest in the job. The most standard approach, of course, is advertising. When you advertise a position opening be sure to do so in the right places and with the right approach. Job ads should appeal to just the type of person you would like to see apply. Don't be surprised if a standard, dull ad in the "Help Wanted" column brings nothing but standard, dull applicants. Sure it's important to be clear about minimum requirements but for just a few dollars more, you can write an ad with some zing to it. Be creative and present the position you have open as the exciting and challenging opportunity that it is. You should aim to sell the library as earnestly as you expect the job candidates to sell themselves.

In order to decide just which newspapers you will advertise in, you need to think about the job itself, the level of special skills or education it requires and the amount of money you will be paying the person in this position. If you are looking to fill a minimum-wage page position that requires little or no prior experience and skills, it really doesn't make much sense to spend a lot of money advertising outside your local area. On the other hand, if you are looking for a professional librarian to become the assistant director, it is worth the added cost to advertise in the larger cities in your state and maybe even in the national professional journals.

In recruiting for any position consider, too, ways to increase the diversity of your staff. The best library service comes from a staff that is as diverse as the community it serves. Consider alternative papers and radio stations. Be sure and place ads in places where you are likely to attract the widest range of applicants.

Don't stop with state or local newspapers and other media outlets, however. Regardless of the position you have open, you'll increase your pool of potential candidates by using every connection you have. With a page position, your very best bet might be a call to the high school guidance counselor. He is in a position to know which students are looking for a part-time job and would be responsible workers. An ad in the school newspaper is another good place to target your search.

In the case of a search for a professional position, contact the state association and the state library as well as the newspapers. Call around to neighboring libraries. Quite often, librarians new to the area or wishing to change jobs will have passed the word around; these agencies and fellow librarians might know about them. Utilize the state library association's website, and post job openings on your own website.

Regardless of the position, the point is the same. Because hiring library staff is one of your most important jobs, it is crucial that you recruit as many qualified applicants as possible to increase your chances of finding the perfect person for the position.

The Selection

Once you have a good pool of applicants you can begin the process of elimination through résumé evaluation, reference checks and interviews. The interview is undoubtedly the best chance you have to evaluate potential candidates, to determine how well each one will fit into the staff and work for the benefit of the library. The interview also sets the stage for your successful candidate's future role at the library. Whether interviewing a potential page or an assistant librarian, you have your first opportunity to show how you value each member of the staff and how you function as a group to serve the public.

Interviews are tough. Remember when you faced your board of trustees for the first time, trying to convince them that you were the perfect person for the job of library director? Try to remember what it was about that interview that made you feel more comfortable, and use that knowledge to help your applicant to relax. You want to get a good feel for the person so that you will be in a better position to judge how effective a staff member he might be.

A good way to begin an interview is to discuss with the applicant *exactly* what the job will entail. Next tell him a little bit about the history of the library and what your goals for service are. By beginning the interview in this way, you accomplish three things: you give the person before you a chance to relax; you provide a clear idea of the responsibilities of the job and how they fit into your overall idea of library services; and you get a chance to gauge the applicant's response to the list of duties as well as to library service in general.

After you have talked about the job and the library a bit and have put the applicant at ease, it's time to turn the interview over to him. Find out a little about this person. Why has he applied for the job? What is it about this job in particular that he finds interesting? Look for spark and enthusiasm: look for signs that this person cares about libraries and is service-oriented.

If the position is for clerk or page duties, you might want to administer a short, standardized filing test. These can be ordered through many different office supply companies. Because accuracy in filing and shelving is so crucial to the smooth functioning of the library, it is important that the applicant, no matter how charismatic, be able to put things in correct alphabetical and numerical order.

If you are hiring a person for a professional position, be sure that the interview includes a substantial discussion of the applicant's library and service philosophy. What is this applicant's commitment to intellectual freedom, to outreach, and to the importance of children's services? Find out where this person stands on such issues as fees for "special" library services and how he envisions the library of the future. These are important matters and you want a feeling of compatibility with your staff on these critical library issues that shape the direction your library takes in providing service. Minor differences of opinion can provoke thought; major philosophical differences will only promote dissension and unhappiness. Find these things out during the interview, not during the first week of the new person's employment.

The interview process should include a tour of the library and, if the position is at a supervisory level, an additional interview with the staff. You may be sold on a particular applicant, but if it's hate at first sight between him and the staff, you may wish to reconsider your preliminary decision. Every library staff has its own group dynamics and in the small library, these dynamics are intensified. One employee's inability to get along with the other members of the staff has an immediate and direct impact on the smooth running of the library as a whole. Be aware that when you hire new staff members, you alter the existing dynamics. You owe it to your staff—and the community—to be responsive to staff opinions and feelings about potential coworkers.

In discussing the merits of the candidates with your staff, be sure you discuss the importance that a diverse workforce can make in the quality of your services. Though you want to build a team that works well together, you want to be sure that this doesn't become an excuse to establish an entrenched homogeneity in your organization. If you've done a good job in sharing the philosophical values that drive librarianship—that is, the importance of equality of services and recognition of the diverse needs of your patrons—it should follow that there is a mutual sense that diversity on staff will enhance these values. Be sure all candidates are respected for the differences and diversity they can bring to the library, as well as for the shared commitment to service that they can also bring.

It has been said that most employers make a decision about an applicant during the first three minutes of an interview. Trusting your instincts is an important component to hiring new employees, but admitting that even you sometimes make mistakes is equally important. Do both the library and the applicant a favor: give him the benefit of the doubt by doing your best to withhold judgment until the interviewing process is complete.

If none of the candidates really has what you are looking for but you are desperate to fill the position *now*, you might try hiring the person who comes closest to meeting your expectations for a trial period of six months to a year. A word of caution, though. If the person doesn't work out, you are going to be in the position of having to let him go when you reopen the search. Even if you have set up a probation period with the understanding that permanent employment may not be offered, letting a new employee go in this manner is still going to be as hard as any employment termination. Facing this unpleasant task (along with facing the prospect of reopening the search) may cause you to make do. In the end, the best advice on hiring is probably never to hire anyone you have reservations about. You are much better off surviving with an unfilled position for a while than to accept a substandard employee and have him until he retires (and I guarantee you, bad employees *never* leave on their own; if this isn't one of Murphy's Laws, it ought to be).

ORIENTATION AND SUPPORT

Once you've hired just the person you'd like to spend the rest of your professional life with, your job is not over. The first thing you will need to do is help the new employee fit into the library's culture. Not only should you be sure that the first week or so is spent sharing your library's values, services, commitments and goals; you should also be sharing your own expectations for performance. This first week is very likely to set the stage for your future together. Don't lose this valuable opportunity to bring the new staff member into the fold and establish a clear understanding of what you expect from him and how he can work successfully with you and the rest of the staff. Take some time to get to know him, and give him a chance to get to know you and the rest of the staff. Take him to lunch; introduce him to regular patrons and members of the Friends and trustees.

It is also helpful to provide a new employee with a special "Orientation Packet" that includes important library policies, a statement of the value you place on staff, a statement of the value of the library in the community, a statement of your support for intellectual freedom. You might also include a list of dates that are important, such as staff meeting days, library hours of operation, bookmobile schedule (if you have one), and times and holidays. This kind of packet will serve as a reminder of what's important to your library and will reinforce your expectations based on library values and principles. (See Appendix B—Orientation Checklist.)

Beyond the initial orientation, the new employee (and this is true of all your employees) will need constant support from you if he is to become and remain a happy and productive worker. There are many ways in which you can support and nurture members of the staff. Offering constructive evaluations on a regular basis, soliciting employees' advice and opinions on library policy and practice, and ensuring their participation in relevant workshops and conferences are all effective ways to help members of the staff grow professionally and become increasingly valuable to the library.

Remember, this new employee is an important asset. You've invested time and money in bringing him on board, as you have with all your staff members. Anything you do to ensure his success is taking a big step forward in ensuring your library's success. Besides, it's just the right thing to do.

THE JOB DESCRIPTION

Nothing will help a staff member succeed better than knowing exactly what's expected of him. This is important at the beginning of a new staff member's tenure and it will be important throughout his career in your library. The job description can and should evolve as your environment changes, but it is always a written document that outlines your expectations in a very objective manner.

In order for employees to be truly effective in their positions, they must be very clear as to what those positions entail and how each one fits into the overall running of the library. This seems obvious enough, but it's amazing how often positions are not clearly defined and how frequently job descriptions are nonexistent. Before you go any further in staff development you must do two things (with the help of your staff): be sure that each position has an up-to-date written job description, and be sure there is a written personnel policy in the hands of every employee.

Job descriptions, if drawn up correctly, are fundamental. They can do much more than offer up a shopping list of duties and responsibilities. If you work with each staff member in preparing the job description, it can be a tool that focuses and defines the employee's work. It is a way to articulate the importance of each job, and it can establish the employee's place in the library as nothing else can.

A good job description should begin with a brief summary of the job and how it relates to other positions in the library as well as its importance to the library as a whole. Then a list of responsibilities should follow specifying exactly which tasks and duties fall under the purview of this position. Take care with the language used in the job description; it should be a reflection of the way you see each position and the way you would like it to be viewed by others. Rather than writing "locks up doors and windows at closing," you might want to put "responsible for building security" followed by a list of examples of what this might mean (for instance, ensuring that all doors and windows are locked upon closing). Instead of "gets plumbing fixed when necessary," try "in charge of facilities maintenance" and, again, list examples of what this might entail. Let the language of your job description reflect the highest degree of responsibility attached to specific duties. A job description is key when budget-makers are determining salaries and raises—don't sell yourself or your employees short. Finally, a job description should include a list of minimum educational and experience requirements as well as a list of desired qualifications.

Many library directors look at job descriptions as just so much burdensome paperwork. If the job description is drawn up by you together with the employee in the position to which it applies, however, it will provide a valuable opportunity for you to discover your respective expectations and how these might differ. Used correctly, a job description can be a creative tool for staff development and employee evaluation. (See Appendix C—Sample Job Description Worksheet.)

Personnel Policies

If you don't already have a written personnel policy, begin work on one now. If you have one, get it out now and review it. A personnel policy should be the document that guides your judgment and decisions regarding staff and the issues that affect them. Working within the larger framework of your town's personnel policy (if it has one which applies to the library), you should work together with your staff in determining the policies that will affect all of you in the library. Although any final document will have to be approved and accepted by the board of trustees, the most effective and fair document is one you have worked on together with suggestions and advice coming from the board of trustees.

On a practical level, the personnel policy will spell out the terms of employment, including such things as a statement of nondiscrimination; hiring practices and authority; employee benefits and compensation; direct assistance (including financial assistance and time off) for staff development through workshops, conferences, and so on; grievance procedures; and termination procedures. For the good of you and your employees, the policies guiding all personnel practices must be in writing. This is especially true if serious personnel problems arise that might require termination.

A personnel policy should be as unique as the institution it's written for but the issues it should address are fairly standard. If you are writing a personnel policy for the first time, check with your town's personnel director as well as with other libraries. Once you've compiled some good examples, you can begin to work with your staff in addressing your own particular needs. (See Appendix D—Personnel Policy Worksheet.)

Continuing Education

The factors that argue for continuing education in the library sector are compelling. Our world is changing rapidly and nowhere more than in the area of information technology. The ways available to us to provide information to the public are evolving constantly, as are the opportunities. In order to make wise decisions about online resources while balancing always too-tight budgets, we must understand our choices well. Library staff members must also be acquainted with the technology that is changing the way we do business and must be able to utilize that growing number of databases and other online resources. Not only that, but library employees who provide public service must know well which resource will work best in supporting a patron's need. Is it a book? A magazine? That database or this website? Library employees working in support services are seeing their jobs change radically as technology expands the way in which we provide patron access and improved technical services.

In addition to the enormous impact that technology is having is the fact that in the world of librarianship in general, and small librarianship in particular, there is a great deal of professional isolation. Add to that the fact that for most of us, the hope for formal continuing education is limited or nonexistent, and you have some great ingredients for stagnation and job burn-out. A good director can stop this from happening, however, in some significant ways. Providing your staff members with opportunities to attend workshops, meetings, and conferences is a great way to reduce isolation and allow your staff to become more knowledgeable about the services they provide as well as to become more skilled. Once every employee understands exactly what is expected of him and knows clearly the terms of employment, the next step is to ensure that the avenue for professional growth is always open.

In order to keep employees challenged and happy in their jobs and to show them that you value them enough to invest in their continuing education, you must *insist* that there is enough money in the budget for staff development. No matter which state you work in, there will be workshops and conferences available to help library employees brush up on old skills and learn new ones, get hands-on experience with and learn about new technology, discuss important library issues with their colleagues, and be rejuvenated professionally. Don't look at this money spent on your staff as a "fringe benefit"; think of it as a necessity for the library. A well-educated staff that has had the opportunity to become familiar with new technology and new perspectives, and has had practical discussions on library issues with colleagues will have a lot more to offer the library than a staff that has become complacent and bored.

Be sure, too, that money is made available each year to buy books and periodicals written for the library profession and then encourage members of the staff to read them—on library time! Who knows better than a librarian the limitless value of the printed word for educating, informing, enlightening and stimulating? Librarian—heal thyself—READ!

While many directors give lip service to the importance of the library staff, many will not fight the good fight for additional staff development revenue. I have seen librarians who will go the distance for new computers or facility improvements and then give the excuse that there is no money in the budget for all interested staff members to attend at least one workshop or conference during the course of the year. Let this be the year to forgo new equipment or new initiatives and get that staff development line item up. Do it now, and do it at the expense of your materials budget if necessary. Your staff needs it and the entire library will benefit enormously as a consequence.

As essential as money is for adequate staff development, there are ways to encourage growth among your employees that will not require a significant amount of funding. If professional isolation and stagnation begin to creep in, you might want to help orchestrate a staff swap with a neighboring library. Consider swapping assistant librarians for a week. The next month exchange children's librarians. The summer might be a good time to let your clerk see how the other half lives—and don't forget yourself. A library staff swap, if handled well, can be an invaluable opportunity for you and your staff to come up with more innovative ways of doing things, streamline old procedures, or just come back feeling lucky you work for *this* library. Just remember that even though this idea is inexpensive, it's not free. If you do organize a swap, realize that you will have to spend time on training and be sure to reimburse participating staff members for mileage.

In addition to traditional and less traditional options within the library world, you should also stay aware of the continuing education opportunities that your town offers to its employees. Investigate, as well, opportunities that come from the private sector and from nonprofit agencies in your area. Many of these options will be available to you and your staff at nominal cost—or even for free. Network with other service providers and find out where the opportunities are. Many of the issues we deal with are not so different from others in both the commercial and nonprofit world. Such areas as strategic planning, customer service, time management, and marketing are common staff development issues. The fact is, we can often learn more from the private sector or other nonlibrary agencies because they have different areas of expertise and different perspectives. Be sure that your employees have access to the widest range of professional development opportunities possible and be creative in seeking them out. In the end, your library services will benefit and your employees will have real opportunities to stay fresh and engaged in their work.

Staff Evaluation

We have all heard the results of studies on motivation that report that positive reinforcement is often more meaningful to employees than salaries—and providing your staff with good feedback is free! As common as this knowledge may be, it seems it is an area that is often overlooked by library directors. How often it is that we hear employees complaining that they never get a formal evaluation or that they never get any feedback at all. It simply isn't fair to someone who comes in to work everyday not to get feedback on how they are doing. It's also a lost opportunity for you to coach and help your staff become even better at their jobs.

You can help staff members avoid stagnation and burn-out through consistent and continual evaluation. Evaluations should be handled in two ways: on a formal basis once a year when you and the staff member compare notes on overall job performance and satisfaction, and on an informal and continuing basis. When evaluations are constructive, most employees value them as guidelines for improvement and support as well as for confirmation of a job well done. Directors, however, often find them uncomfortable and maybe even nonproductive. Because you owe it to your staff, your library and yourself to evaluate the performance of those who work for you, it is important for you to devise a method of formal evaluation that will be meaningful and easy to administer.

The formal, once-a-year evaluation can be as creative or standard as you want it to be. However it is done, it should be based on mutually agreed upon goals for performance that you've already established. Based on the employee's job description as well as on the personal and professional goals you've discussed in the past, the evaluation should assess the degree to which the employee has succeeded in meeting those goals. Choose a method that you feel comfortable with, because unless you can speak as freely about areas that need improvement as you can about the areas in which the employee excels, the benefit of your evaluation will be limited.

One effective method involves asking each employee to write down (before your meeting) the areas where he feels he might need improvement and those areas about which he is most proud. How well does he feel he's accomplished previously set goals? In what ways can you or the library help him meet his goals better in the future? What plans does he have for future growth? Give the employee an opportunity to assess the library's culture and policies that enable or create barriers to workplace achievement. Take this opportunity to ask him for ideas for improving the workplace to make it more effective for staff performance.

Prior to your formal evaluation meeting, you should identify, in writing, areas for improvement as well as areas you feel are exemplary. How well has this employee met the goals you agreed upon at the last evaluation? Has the environment changed enough to change the priorities of the goals or even render them moot? If so, how has this employee changed with the changing workplace to ensure that the values inherent in the predetermined goals were honored? Comparing notes can be most enlightening. You will have a chance to verify that you are both on the same page in terms of expectations and perceived accomplishments. This is the right time to set new goals upon which the employee will be evaluated during the course of the ensuing year.

Of course, the annual evaluation should hold no surprises for anyone if you've been doing your job well all year long. That is, as director you should be giving informal evaluations constantly. Nothing works like instant gratification or, in some cases, instant correction. Throughout the year, your employees will give you plenty of opportunity to praise their work. Do it often. It's free, and it means more to most people than almost anything else you can provide. As the director, you get plenty of positive reinforcement from the community; pass it along! You get that praise because of the fine job you *and* your staff are doing.

By the same token, if an employee's performance is not measuring up to your expectations, tell him immediately. Let him know exactly what your expectations are and find out if you are in agreement as to what needs to be changed and how it should be done. Don't let a lack of communication get in the way of good job performance on the part of your staff. An immediate, private discussion with a staff member who is having trouble performing his job will reinforce your mutual goals and clarify your expectations.

I know of one case, for example, when the director noticed that a certain employee seemed to be on the phone an inordinate amount of time. This director was irritated by the personal phone calls but didn't discuss the matter with the employee right away. I think this director felt that he was overreacting, that this was really no big deal. As time passed, however, the employee's calls seemed to become more and more frequent and the employee was ignoring the work that needed to be done.

Finally the director blew up. He told his employee that there were to be absolutely no more personal calls unless there was a bona fide emergency. The employee was dumbfounded. What brought this on "all of a sudden"? The employee lost respect for such a "tyrannical" and unreasonable boss and the director lost respect for an employee who didn't have enough sense to realize she should *work* while at work.

The real tragedy of this case is that it was so avoidable. If the director had discussed his concerns with the employee as soon as they became concerns, they could have hit upon an agreement for phone calls that made sense for both of them. In the end, the director was guilty of the very thing he was trying to avoid at the beginning—over-reacting. Constructive criticism may be difficult for many of us but saving it up for the annual evaluation is only going to allow the situation to deteriorate, leaving the employee to feel (rightly) that it was *your* responsibility to have let him know about it when it first happened.

To be successful in staff development, you should look at the members of the staff as the valuable resources they are. If they don't have something important to contribute, they shouldn't be there. If they are there, use them. Members of the staff have much more to offer than their time; they have their minds. The most progressive, community-responsive libraries have more than one person contributing to their management; they have the entire staff. If you don't think the high school kid coming in to shelve books could possibly come up with an idea to make the job better, think again. That person is *just* the one to have thoughts on making the job better. Consulting the page on how this or other library services might be improved can only get you two things: a better way of doing things and a happier employee who knows that his opinions count for something.

In the small library, consultative management may be the best technique. This is management that stems from good communication with every member of the staff. Good communication keeps ideas rolling in—some good, some bad, but rolling in just the same. Consultative management depends on regular staff meetings and informal talks with staff members throughout the week. In the end, decisions regarding the running of the library are yours; that's as it should be. Remember, however, that you are just one person with one mind and your ability to make smart decisions and establish responsible direction for your library will be enhanced immeasurably with continual input from the staff.

You are the director. As such you do not act in every scene, instead you are responsible for establishing the direction in which the library should head. Those working for the director are the ones who are actually onstage performing the functions necessary to make that happen. It's true that in small libraries the director might be needed to participate in such things as working at the front desk (an enlightening job, especially if you are interested in how well you are really serving the public—all library directors should do this on occasion), or taking charge of storytime when the children's librarian calls in sick. Regardless of the tasks that need to be performed by the director to keep the books circulating and the library running smoothly, the most important role is the one of establishing goals for service, providing vision and working with the staff to turn that vision into reality.

The Problem Employee

Okay, let's say you're perfect. You know you'll do a splendid job in hiring new staff members when the time comes; you are committed to staff development and giving ongoing support and encouragement. Even the best managers, however, aren't immune to that employee who just isn't going to measure up. Despite all your best efforts at coaching, reinforcing, and corrective actions, some employees just don't belong in libraries. When you've done everything you can, the responsible next move is to fire this staff member.

It is important to keep a good clear paper trail on all the corrective actions you've taken. Be sure that your coaching sessions with the employee have been documented. Be brave and honest and let the problem employee know he is on probation and must improve or will have to go. Be very explicit about what is wrong and what must be done to improve. It is important that you are clear that you are seeking consistent high-level performance (again, give this in writing to the employee—see below) and that further failure to meet this level will result in termination. This is a tough thing to do, but trust me, it is much easier than living with a substandard employee for what seems like forever. And the longer you wait to take strong corrective action, the harder it gets.

In addition, there is often that problem employee that you've inherited (and doesn't everyone)? All the library directors before you were gutless wonders, allowing this person to hang on, feeling little guilt (and tremendous relief) at passing him off on you. Even as a new director, you will likely spot a problem employee right away (or will have this person identified for you by frustrated staff who hope you can finally do something about him). If you are new, you will most likely be feeling that a little time should pass before you begin making any changes as drastic as firing someone.

Being new means you don't, as yet, know where loyalties lie. A longtime employee may be someone the public has come to tolerate, even if this person is obnoxious and rude. Chances are that simply due to longevity he will be perceived by the public as having rights that a young (or not so young) upstart such as you has no business trampling on. A new director would be wise to generate a little loyalty and trust among the public, the staff and the board of trustees before making any major changes. The library has gotten along thus far in whatever degree of efficiency without your changes; it can continue to do so for another few months. One caveat, though, don't wait too long or your inaction may well be seen as acceptance.

Because the firing of an employee can be a very traumatic experience for everyone involved, it makes sense to explore every avenue open to turn the problem employee around. In the past, poor management may have been the problem. Therefore, you could make the initial assumption that with your own management style and expertise you may be able to turn this employee into a happy and productive member of the staff. If after several months you see no improvement, however, it may be time for some serious soul-searching.

How do you honestly rate yourself as an employer? Remember, your job is to direct the other employees and, hopefully, you have been doing just that. You should be sure that an employee who is failing at his job does not mean that you are failing at yours. Go back to the issue of staff development. Are you really giving this employee the guidance and encouragement he needs? Have you specifically spelled out your expectations and discussed how they might best be carried out? If you can honestly say that the problems do not lie either with you or with your communication with the employee, it's time to look at the specific areas of concern you have with the employee in question.

Once you have identified the areas of unacceptable behavior or the problem with a particular employee, make an annotated list, explaining clearly (both for yourself and for the employee) what is unacceptable, what type of behavior or performance should replace it, and how this might be accomplished. As hard as it might be for you to confront a fellow worker with what you perceive to be his inadequacies, it is both necessary and fair. As soon as you have stated the case, you must have an interview with the employee. Because it should be assumed that this person wants to do a good job, wants to keep the job, and was a good employee at one time, you might begin the interview by asking: "Are you satisfied with your position here?" By asking this question, you will be letting the employee know that you care and that you are assuming there is some explanation for the poor performance you have observed.

Be prepared for any response. You may open yourself up to an entire shopping list of continual crises in this person's life, enough pain and agony to fill an entire week of daytime television. While major (and even minor) personal problems will affect even the most stalwart of individual's work performance, there is a limit to how long any place of employment should tolerate substandard achievement from its workers, regardless of personal circumstance. This might be construed as a pretty tough statement, but as director your responsibility is to the well-being of the library as a whole.

The employee might also respond with a long list of grievances about the operation of the library itself which for any number of reasons have been kept under wraps until now. These grievances may be things that can be worked out. Low pay, low esteem, boredom, or fellow employees might be among the problems. Of these, low pay may be the only thing over which you have no immediate control. The others should not exist if you do your job of staff development and direction effectively.

If the employee cites low pay as the culprit, you should be very clear that short of cost-of-living increases, meritorious performance is required for raises. It's all too true that library salaries are notoriously poor and it's important that as director, you work continuously on making the case for higher wages. The bottom line, however, is that you have a virtual contract with your employees. You agree to hire at a certain rate of pay, and they agree to perform according to expectations and in accordance with the job description. If there is legitimate concern over that rate of pay, you should expect your employees to discuss this with you honestly so that, together, you can work out a solution. Simply reducing the quality of the work an employee does for the library is never an option you should tolerate. Realize, however, that if, indeed, the salary structure is so low that it is adversely impacting staff performance, you have a much bigger problem to deal with and this may only be the first symptom to surface (see Chapter One).

It's just as likely that when asked if satisfied in the job, the problem employee will respond with a simple "yes." In this case, it's up to you to say that the performance you have observed is below your expectations and that you wondered whether it was due to some aspect of the job he was having trouble with. What should ensue, in any case, is a very clear discussion of what you expect, how it might be achieved, and when you expect to see results.

Give the employee a copy of a list of areas where you expect to see improvement, and keep a copy for yourself. Make an appointment for a follow-up interview at which time two things should happen: there should be a reappraisal of the employee's performance with any improvements noted, and there should be a chance for him to respond to your list after having had the opportunity to give it some thought. It seems reasonable to wait about two weeks. Any more time and you are likely to let the situation drop; any less time is insufficient for him to show marked improvement and to evaluate his own performance.

Be sure that you keep a record of your talks with this employee. Keep dates of your discussions as well as the copy of the list you gave him citing problem areas and indicating clearly what will happen if there isn't sufficient improvement. It will also be wise to write down after the interview how the discussion went and your opinion of the employee's receptivity to the discussion.

Although nobody wants an employee who must be watched continually, for the next couple of weeks you should monitor his performance carefully, not just to correct it (do so immediately—yet privately—if necessary), but to encourage and assist. A cheering section of one might be just what this person needs, and if you begin to see some improvement, gradually give the employee more rein. In the end, you want staff members who work well without someone constantly looking over their shoulders.

Perhaps there is an interim solution for the problem employee. Depending on the circumstances, a leave of absence may be the answer. There are times when serious personal problems (e.g., illness in the family, marital difficulties, child in trouble) or job burn-out is at the bottom of unacceptable work performance. Both you and your employee should consider this option if it seems likely that extended time off will correct the problems, where behavior modification has not worked. One obvious difficulty with this plan is money. If you are unable or unwilling to offer a paid leave of absence, or if vacation time is insufficient, you may have to insist on an unpaid leave of absence. Be sure, however, that in taking this route you are on solid legal ground, have systematically reviewed and evaluated the employee's performance, and have given these evaluations in writing to the employee. It is important, too, to discuss this possible plan of action with your board of trustees and perhaps with your town's personnel director as well.

As too many library directors know, there are some employees who cannot be changed, motivated or moved to a new area where they might be productive and not disruptive. You've done everything you can but the problem employee does not change. You've carefully documented each formal talk you've had with this person and have outlined in writing (one copy for each of you) what is lacking in his performance and what must be done to correct it. You've had follow-up sessions which you've documented and no improvement has been forthcoming. You know he's got to go. The time has come.

The overwhelming temptation may be to take the ostrich approach: ignore it and maybe it will go away. It won't of course, but I think it's okay to take this route for just a few days. It's a little like buying a lottery ticket. The likelihood of your winning is extremely slim; what you are really purchasing is some short-term hope. In addition, the ostrich approach will give you a few more days to face up to what you have to do, consult your personnel policy to be sure you have covered all your bases, and to explore the most painless way to handle the soon-to-be ex-employee.

It's important to keep in mind that the firing of an employee who has no business working in the library is the responsible thing to do. It is part of what you were hired for. Furthermore, although nothing is going to make this situation pleasant for the fired employee, you may be doing something constructive for him in the long run. Obviously this person was not meant to work in libraries or at least not in your library. This action may cause some serious self-evaluation and perhaps head him in a new and more fulfilling direction. It might also be that the problem employee was asking for it, literally, albeit subconsciously. If the employee has become so nonproductive that you must fire him, if the employee has failed to respond to any support, guidance, or encouragement you've given, then it might be because he actually wants out but can't bring himself to make the break.

It's hard to imagine that anything is going to make this final interview easy. You can, however, make it just a little less difficult by having firmly in mind exactly what you are going to say. It might help to write up a script and rehearse it (this has the added benefit of reinforcing just how right you are in taking this action, especially if you're beginning to get cold feet). If you're not comfortable with a script, then consider an outline either written or firmly set in your mind of just how you came to this decision. Remind the employee of your past expectations, given in writing. Remind him that subsequent guidance and encouragement brought about no appreciable change. Tell him that your job is to ensure the best quality of service to the public, and since his performance was not up to your articulated standards, you have decided this move is necessary.

Be as compassionate in your language and explanations as you can possibly be, but be firm. Promises and protestations may tempt you to change your mind but don't. It would only make the termination more difficult next time—and, believe me, there will be a next time.

My best advice is to ask the employee to leave as soon as he is able to clear his desk and gather his belongings. If the employee's transgressions weren't illegal or immoral, I would also offer a minimum of two weeks' severance pay. It is very painful to insist that an employee leave right away but there is absolutely nothing to be gained by allowing this staff member to hang around even for a week or two. First, he may well campaign hard and perhaps even successfully to be reinstated—putting you right back at square one and making the next round even harder. Second, a lame-duck employee will create a very difficult work environment either by bad-mouthing you or by generating sympathy for his plight which may turn others into problem employees.

No matter how well you handle the situation, and regardless of how justified, firing an employee can be one of the hardest challenges facing anyone. No matter how cold your blood or hard your heart, you are bound to lose sleep over it. The relief you feel when the employee leaves, however, and the immediate benefits you and the library reap when a capable and enthusiastic person comes in as a replacement, will more than compensate you. You'll wonder in just a few days' time what took you so long.

Volunteers

It is hard to imagine running a small library without volunteers. In fact, in the very small library it is quite likely that volunteers outnumber paid staff. Volunteers can offer a library even more than their time, as valuable as that is. Your volunteers will have a vested interest in the health and vitality of the library. They will be among your most dependable supporters when you need to convince town government of your financial needs. In fact, who better to send that message than those who love the library enough to donate their time and energy to provide service? When the chips are down, they will be there for you.

Because the volunteer workforce is (or should be) a critical asset to the small library, it is important that they are well managed to maximize their value and their potential to help you deliver excellent services. In managing volunteers, the view is often espoused that "Volunteers in the library should be recruited, evaluated and in all other respects, treated just as you would paid employees." Those of us who actually *do* manage volunteers know that nothing could be further from the feasible. Let's face a fact right now that makes it nearly impossible for directors of small public libraries to treat volunteers like paid employees: they're *not* paid! Although volunteers are people from the community who love the library and want to contribute to it, they are not accountable, and without that paycheck, it is very hard to make them accountable. Managing volunteers presents some unique challenges.

Criticizing and correcting job performance takes on a whole new light and requires special tact. For instance, demanding strict adherence to a schedule with vacation guidelines spelled out will probably discourage some volunteer services. Yet these are important components to the smooth running of the library. Because managing volunteers can get pretty sticky, there may be a temptation to do without them. Even if you can get along without their services financially, there are important extrabudgetary reasons to welcome the service of community citizens.

Volunteers bring the library so much more than their labor. For example, volunteers can offer wonderful new perspectives and may offer unique ideas for service delivery. It is quite possible that in a small library, volunteers give our staffs the greatest diversity in terms of background, age, and life experience. It would be a real waste not to capitalize on this. As creative as we may believe we are in designing and delivering service, we who have chosen this profession are likely to be constrained by our own experience and knowledge. Volunteers who come from all walks of life can broaden our perspectives. In addition, volunteers will come with a "patron's" perspective and may be able to help us improve our services because they know, as patrons, what is best about our services and what might be changed to make them better.

Another critically important role volunteers can and do play for the library is that of citizen advocate. Who better to support the library than someone who gives freely to deliver services? And who better to accurately send the message about the library's needs than an "insider" who really knows how important financial support is for the library? Your volunteers will send the message of the library's importance in informal ways—for instance, through casual word of mouth at other venues in which they participate—and often formally by speaking out at budget time. Importantly, their voices on the library's behalf are enhanced immeasurably by the fact that they have put their "time" where their mouths are.

Finally, bringing volunteers into the library will show those who fund you that you are sharing in the "costs" of running the library. When you make your case at budget time, the town leaders are likely to want to know how you are helping yourselves. You can talk about grants and gifts and ... you can talk about volunteers! Be sure to keep track of all your volunteers' hours and calculate their time contribution in dollars.

While it is clear that volunteers are very important to libraries in many ways, it is critically important that they form only an *auxiliary* labor force. That is, volunteers should supplement paid staff; they should not replace them. If your budget is inadequate to support the staff you need, you will have to address the problem of the budget (see Chapter One). If you attempt to round out an inadequate work force with volunteers, you will lose the best bargaining chip you have to get the increased funding you need. No one is going to pay for something they can get for free. Even if you have a perfect volunteer in a position that ordinarily would be paid, you will pay for his services dearly when he leaves. It will be very hard to convince the town government that in addition to the usual increases, you need to add a new paid staff position as well. You may get the money you need, but if you don't, you'll be left with a hole in your staff that may be impossible to fill again with a volunteer.

When assessing the value of volunteers, do not make the mistake of assuming they are free. Volunteers take training, and in many cases significantly more supervision than staff. You can maximize their value to your library by ensuring that you provide a very thorough and professional orientation for new volunteers. Develop job descriptions for your volunteers so it is clear what you expect of them (see Appendix E—Volunteer Job Description). Assign a member of the staff or a veteran volunteer to be a mentor for the first month of a new volunteer's service—this will not only improve their training, it will also make them feel more at home and help them become integrated into the library's culture more quickly. Finally, be sure a new volunteer understands the goals and mission of your library. A volunteer will often work only a couple of hours a week so the training and orientation they get in the beginning of their service will help tremendously in ensuring the highest quality performance in the years to come.

When considering volunteers, don't forget the children's services. Quite often, the children's room is the busiest place in the library; volunteers can make a tremendous contribution here. If you shake the right trees (try the Parent Teacher Association or the school newsletter), you may find someone who is great at storytelling or who has some background in children's services. Be sure, however, to spell out your requirements. If you want someone with some education in children's literature, say so. Present the volunteer opportunity in the exciting light it deserves. You might be surprised at the number of people with education backgrounds who would love to make a contribution to the library while their children are in school. You might also get lucky and find a retired person who misses working with children.

One caveat: No matter how desperate you may be for help in the children's room, remember that the people who work there will be contributing to the creation of a lifelong image of libraries for the children. Make sure that image is a good one by ensuring that everyone who works in the children's room (paid or not) clearly enjoys children.

BRINGING VOLUNTEERS ON BOARD

Very often volunteers will come to you. Patrons who use the library and have some time on their hands often provide the bulk of a volunteer crew. If you are serious about increasing your volunteer staff, however, it will be important to be aggressive in recruiting them. If you take the initiative, you are likely to get the caliber of volunteer you need, and you can increase the variety of talent as well as the diversity of your staff.

Consider your volunteer needs. If your goal is to increase both your volunteer force and support for your library, you may wish to go outside the bounds of your traditional support base. A notice in church bulletins or a small ad in the help-wanted column of your local paper should do the trick. Once again, it is important to have firmly in mind what it is you wish from your new volunteers and what the minimum requirements for the job are. Spell these out in your recruitment efforts and you will have a better chance of eliminating unsuitable volunteers from the outset.

Also think about the kinds of people and talent you are looking for. If you need someone for a very specific project—working to promote library services, for example—you may want to approach the local business community for volunteer assistance. If you are looking for help in organizing your local history collection and making it more accessible to the public, you might consider talking to local history organizations to see if they would take the library's local history collection on as their own project. Whenever you have these sorts of specialized opportunities, however, it will be critically important for you to work closely with the volunteers at the outset to be sure they understand clearly the parameters of the work. A public relations specialist helping you design marketing materials will need to be clear about your library's message. A group of history buffs will have to understand how the local history collection fits in with the rest of your collection and that its organization is consistent with all your library's resources.

When you think about expanding your volunteer staff, don't forget teen volunteers. Teens do require special handling and may not be as consistent as older volunteers, but they bring with them a level of energy and enthusiasm that is unmatched. In addition, giving teens fun volunteer opportunities is a great way to encourage this otherwise hard-to-reach group to use the library. If you want someone to help in the children's room, you might consider teen volunteers as mentors for grade school children. Think about going to some of the high school service clubs and see if you can interest some teens in donating time to the library.

THE PERFECT MATCH

If you work with volunteers you know that not all volunteers really have the skills they need to be effective in traditional volunteer jobs. If you give it some thought, however, you are likely to come up with something that the "less than perfect" volunteers can do. It can be the simplest of tasks (straightening out the reading room, putting pockets in books before they're covered, typing overdue notices, and so on)—and you don't have to schedule them for more than a couple hours a month.

In addition to volunteers who have limited skills, there are also volunteers who, over time, become less and less proficient at what they do. Sometimes a lateral move in the library can be handled with grace and satisfaction for both you and the volunteer. Sometimes, however, volunteers (being human beings) can be stubborn about where they are willing to put in their time and in-house job changes just won't work. Perhaps the point can best be made by example.

In my first job as library director I was guilty of harboring a totally unsuitable volunteer in the library. At workshops and conferences I discussed my volunteer problem and was invariably told by workshop leaders and educators that mine was a difficult and unique problem. (It's interesting that when fellow librarians heard my story they usually commiserated with me because they had similar problems.)

The volunteer in question (I'll call her Marie) had been at the library for uncounted years (I inherited her but do not blame my predecessor—she would look to me today like the perfect library volunteer if I didn't know better). Marie used to work at a large public library in California—a fact that she liked to remind us of all the time. It was there that she learned much about the operations of a public library. She saw library automation at its very beginning and clearly understood its boon to the profession. She needed only a short description of how we wanted a job done, and she was on her way. Her follow-through was great; giving her a long-term project always meant getting it done and done well.

Because of her library background, she understood the whys of projects and was, therefore, very quick to understand the hows. She was a prominent member of the community and outspoken in her belief that the library should be an important priority in the dispensing of tax money. She herself had given generously to the library to buy special equipment and supplies we would not otherwise have been able to afford.

A treasure, right? Well ... not exactly. Marie had an extraordinarily obnoxious manner. Not one member of the staff liked to work with her, and I don't believe there was one patron who had gone without being chastised by her for some real or imagined transgression against the library or the library's policies. You see, Marie did not come to us without strings. She extracted a promise from my predecessor (who made the pledge because she was understandably anxious to secure such a knowledgeable and capable worker) that she would be allowed to work at the circulation desk a few hours each week. Small price, you say? Marie was truly unpleasant to all who crossed her path.

Believe me, I tried everything to remove Marie from duty at the front desk. I told her honestly how valuable her library knowledge was to us for such things as sorting through gift books, completing interlibrary loan requests, making book inventories, and performing other special library projects. If she really wanted to help us out, I said, she would give up her time on the desk and put it to more valuable use tackling those projects only a volunteer with her important library background could complete. Her answer was simple and firm. "I'm happy to help you out with any special project; you know how much libraries mean to me. But the one job I could never give up is working at the front desk. It's my real reason for being so actively involved with the library. I love working with the public." (Boy, try telling that to the people who cowered before her every Tuesday morning, wondering what it was they had done wrong this time!)

Was the solution simply to tell her that she wasn't suited to the front desk, that there were others who seemed to get on better with the public? She wouldn't have believed it. If I had been successful in getting her to retire from the front desk, it would have been at the expense of her valuable service in other library projects, but more importantly, it would have been at the expense of general library-public good-will.

You see, Marie was not an evil person. She was a woman who at age 75 had become grumpy and unpleasant and didn't even realize it. She truly did love the library and she had been a very important political supporter when we needed it most. In our small town, the reverberations from what could only have been a negative encounter (since she outright rejected a lateral move in the library) would probably have cost us more than the pinched image she presented at the front desk.

We came up with the only solution that made sense for us. We made sure that a staff member was on duty with Marie whenever she worked at the front desk. This staff member worked as mediator between Marie and any of her victims. Through lots of smiling and a little body language (all carried out discreetly while Marie did her thing) we managed to convey to the patrons that we really were a pleasant place and after all, nobody's perfect. Not ideal, I grant you. And I'm sure there are those who would say that Marie was perpetuating that negative image we're all trying hard to dispel. It's true, she was. But remember, she was an elderly woman who had contributed a lot to the community and to the library. She was a friend in need and those who knew her, knew that she meant well. In our case, she'd given countless hours of invaluable service to the library. Forcing her out didn't seem to be a viable solution. Volunteer management is definitely more art than science!

Because public service is so very important, it may be the best solution overall to reconsider the use of library volunteers at the circulation desk. As stated earlier, volunteers should not replace paid staff. If you don't have enough staff members to adequately cover circulation, you need to make that case to your funders. Many small libraries deliver reference services from the circulation desk—either by design or because patrons simply ask their questions of the library staff member who is handiest. We can spend the time to train staff to handle reference requests either by providing the service, or by understanding when a request is complex enough to require assistance from the librarian. Well-meaning volunteers are likely to try to answer reference questions and may even fail to realize when a question is more complex than it appears. Because training for this job is fairly significant and in-depth, it's not a job for volunteers. It is best in the end to find other than direct public services jobs for volunteers.

While I contend there is no perfect solution for the management of the Maries and other challenging volunteers found in small libraries throughout the country, there is a way to get the right volunteer in the right job from the beginning. Here the admonition to treat volunteers like paid staff becomes more possible. Through the interview process you have the opportunity to avoid many future problems. Again, it might be very difficult to flatly turn down an applicant who wants to help out. You can, however, put any willing volunteer in a position that will aid the library and avoid unpleasantries. If a person applies and you're lucky enough to know (or even have a hunch) that he will not generate good-will at the front desk, there are undoubtedly back-room tasks that he could do—covering books, filing catalog cards, typing up overdue notices or book orders, for instance.

One way to determine the suitability of volunteers for various tasks is to get them to fill out a special volunteer application-aptitude form before putting them to work. (See Appendix F—Volunteer Application Form.) This not only helps you place the volunteer in a mutually beneficial location in the library, it also gives you something to refer to if a person insists that he wants to work only at the front desk. Here you will have to stick to your guns and say that according to the "objective" criteria provided on the application form, the best location is the one you've assigned. Be careful not to hedge by saying there is nothing at the desk *now*. If this volunteer then takes you up on your back-room position, he will know when someone *is* needed at the front desk and will be the first to volunteer, putting you in an uncomfortable position.

Another effective way to maintain control over the quality of a volunteer's performance is to make it clear from the very beginning of his employment that you expect him to adhere to the schedule you've agreed upon, giving ample notice if he can't come in. Explain how important it is to have workers you can rely on. This is the best time to let the volunteer know that you value him as much as you do the paid staff and, therefore, it is important for him to follow the same rules as everyone else. It will be helpful when problems arise if you've already established what acceptable work performance means and that you may have to replace a volunteer who is unreliable. Be sure he agrees with the terms of his volunteer employment, and get the agreement in writing.

Finally, be sure that you give each volunteer plenty of feedback. It's easier to correct small mistakes right away than to have to address major performance problems later. Similarly, positive reinforcement is extremely effective, especially when given sincerely and whenever it is deserved. Don't forget to include all your volunteers in the annual evaluation process. Treating volunteers as much like staff as possible in this respect will help them grow and develop into real assets of the library.

Regardless of your particular volunteer situation, remember that you're the boss. You know what is best for the library. While I can't imagine turning down a potential volunteer altogether (the PR ramifications of that could be significant and, besides, someone who is generous enough to want to help the library deserves the opportunity), you are perfectly correct to locate that person where *you* need him, not necessarily where that volunteer wants to be. It is, in fact, your responsibility to do so.

EXPRESSING YOUR APPRECIATION

The best payment you can make to your volunteers is letting them know how important they are to the library. Volunteers provide such a valuable service to libraries by generating good public relations and by helping you to increase the quality of your service. It's important, therefore, to let them know how grateful you are. This should go without saying, of course, but in our busy daily lives, it's easy to take things and people for granted. Be sure that when it comes to volunteers, you make a habit of providing them with feedback. Use positive reinforcement and lots of it. If it isn't too much trouble for volunteers to work for you, it shouldn't be too much trouble for you to compliment them on work performed, to mention how much you've come to depend on their services, and to say thanks often.

In addition to the informal pats on the back, there are some wonderful ways to say thanks in a more formal manner. How about a "Volunteer of the Month" column in your in-house newsletter or the local paper? Ask your Friends group if they would be willing to sponsor an annual volunteer appreciation day complete with lunch or dinner and maybe even an awards ceremony. The staff itself can show its appreciation by inviting the volunteers to a holiday party that the entire staff puts together, where maybe small gifts could be given. The ways to give your volunteers the recognition and thanks they deserve are limited only by your imagination, and whenever you make the gesture, you will be a hero.

THREE

The Library's Collection

Although collection development has changed dramatically and become a lot more complex over the years, I believe that it is as it always has been the very heart of what we do. Obviously, our collection is our raison d'être. Even if playing politics and finessing personnel problems is not your particular cup of tea, what book-loving, access-promoting, true-blue librarian could dislike collection development? Choosing which books and other materials to make available is our true gift to the public and our legacy to the future. Now that job has become even more challenging as we must stretch our materials budget to cover audiovisual formats that continue to change along with a growing number of online resources.

Certainly, developing a good collection that meets the needs of your community is tricky business, and the growing and changing nature of formats makes collection development even trickier. The fact that small libraries have small materials budgets makes the business trickier still. Because of this, the decision is not only which titles to buy but which format to invest in. Given this, how do you decide which books to purchase, which online databases to subscribe to, which video to make available? Do you invest in each new technology—DVDs for example—or do you wait to see which the public wants most? These choices can be difficult, and your decisions will not only impact the quality of your collection today, but also what your patrons of tomorrow are able to find on your shelves. Collection development is much easier if you have a good knowledge of your community's needs and desires along with a judicious selection policy.

Selection Policies

Every library should have a carefully considered collection development policy that clearly and succinctly states the library's selection criteria: how selections are made, what will be included in the collection, and what won't. Be sure that you spell out in very clear terms who is responsible for making selection decisions. If the children's librarian is responsible for selecting all materials in the children's room, say so. If the director is in charge of the adult collection and reference collection, put it in writing. This authority, along with a statement on how objections will be handled, will come in handy if an item comes under fire—or, perhaps even more importantly, if a group or individual wishes to have an item *included* in the collection.

GUIDING PRINCIPLES FOR COLLECTION DEVELOPMENT

You should state in fairly broad terms what areas will be addressed as you purchase materials—for instance books for children, young people and adults; fiction and nonfiction; materials that entertain, inform, instruct, provoke thought, and address issues.

You might state that you will attempt to collect materials in a broad range of subject areas but will give special consideration to materials in particular areas including those that have important regional significance (for example, if you have no historical society making local history materials available).

Finally, all selection policies should have a statement of nondiscrimination. It should be spelled out in your selection policy that materials will not be excluded for selection "because of the race or nationality or the social, political, or religious views of the authors." (See Appendix G—Library Bill of Rights.)

Audiovisual Materials

Audiovisual (AV) materials such as videos and audio cassettes have had a tremendous impact on library use. As libraries began to diversify their formats, they found that they were able to appeal to a much wider clientele. In fact, many libraries with rich collections of books-on-tape and popular videos see that these collections have a much higher turnover rate for a longer period of time than even the most popular fiction. This, of course, can be a rather mixed blessing. The truth is, AV materials tend to have a much shorter life span than the book. Not only do they break and wear out faster, the patron "consumes" this collection a lot more rapidly than the book collection and it is a costly monster to feed! The better your AV collection, the higher the demand. The higher the demand, the more your collection development budget must stretch to cover that demand.

Though I would not advocate serious restrictions on what you purchase once these collections are put in place, I do think there are ways to manage the cost of these highly used (and used up) collections. First, let me say a word about "popular" videos. Some libraries have chosen to stick with educational AV materials and for seemingly good reason. Popular videos, they claim, are cheaply available elsewhere. Why compete with the private sector? What the library can offer that is unique is a collection of special educational videos that might not be available elsewhere. On the surface, this makes sense. But here's a challenge: Go into any library with an educational video collection and try to find one item that doesn't need dusting due to the length of time it has sat, untouched, on the library shelf. While I think a good, small quality collection of educational videos on important and timely topics is a good idea (how-tos on parenting, small business management, and public speaking come to mind), the public primarily looks to videos for leisure entertainment and stimulation. Why not give them this at the library?

You can provide a good popular collection and stay within your budget by developing a good solid working policy for decision-making. Consider being extremely selective about the popular videos you do choose. You might limit your collection to Academy Award winning videos (this way you have popular videos but are also establishing a historic video archive of movies recognized by our most popular award as "best"). Pick only films considered blockbusters, and those independent movies that get exceptional critical acclaim but very little exposure—especially in small towns where movie houses can't afford to bring other than those films that are sure to be commercial successes. Let the patrons help with collection and consider "patron demand" as part of the selection criteria. Look for films that are particularly good representations of particular genres. By drawing up a list of guiding principles for selection, you will be able to create an excellent collection that is high quality and in high demand.

You can also stretch that collection development dollar by being a smart consumer. Wait until the bloom (and high price tag) is off a blockbuster before you purchase it. Check with local video stores and see if they will sell you used videos in good condition once their demand has declined. You'd be surprised at how willing they might be—especially if they know that you are waiting for them to get all the mileage (and bucks) out of a new title before you buy it to offer for free lending at your library.

Buying popular titles on books-on-tape is less questioned as a reasonable approach than videos, but they are just as expensive to purchase and our patrons do go through them quickly. Most libraries have made the decision to stick with unabridged tapes and it's been my experience that the patrons prefer them. Again, developing guidelines for selection of this important collection can help to manage the costs. You might try to complement your print collection by focusing more on the books that are more challenging to read. How many times do we hear from our patrons that they would love to read the latest scholarly biography on a popular person but only have time for the lighter fare of Grisham or Grafton? Because most listen to a book-on-tape while engaged in other activities, they'll appreciate having the chance to listen to a book they would otherwise never have found time to read. In addition, let the patrons help guide you. Since they will usually have access to the book as well as to the tape that your library might offer, try to find from them which titles they're most likely to read themselves, and which they'd rather listen to.

More and more libraries are also beginning to offer music CDs. This is another materials budget-eating monster for sure. Perhaps even more than videos and books-on-tape, patrons are likely to take home armloads of music CDs at a time and come back for more within a few short weeks. Before you know it, they are clamoring for larger and larger collections. In addition, the formats for music seem to change more frequently than for videos and books-on-tape. Over a relatively short period of time we've had LPs, 8-tracks, cassettes, and now compact discs. Coming down the pike are DVDs and by the time this book is five years old, there will probably be another new format. How does a library keep up with changing formats, high patron demands, and a plethora of genres? If you are planning to offer music, you will again have to develop a set of guidelines. As with other AV formats, it makes sense to be sure that if you are going to spend this money at all, the collection is popular enough that you get a lot of circulation out of it. If you decide to stick with one genre (classical, for example) be sure it is a genre that has the widest appeal to the most diverse clientele possible (and be ready to field lots of complaints that you don't have jazz, popular, soundtracks, the blues, and so on).

In addition to the financial costs of AV materials, they also cost libraries in terms of space and shelving. Be sure that this collection is housed in a visible location that keeps it secure (AV materials tend to be much more susceptible to theft than print collections). Also, because these collections tend to be "browsed" you will need shelving that presents them in an eye-catching way. No spine out, bottom shelf housing for this collection!

With all the "costs" involved, it may be tempting to decide to forego audiovisual materials altogether. It is tempting but it would indeed be turning your back on some of the most popular of all public library collections. Times have certainly changed. It's hard to imagine that anyone these days could make a case for a popular book collection but deny the legitimacy of a popular AV collection. With the growing diversity of formats in this new digital age, it's important that public libraries respond to them so that they are seen as relevant. Because these collections are so popular, they make a great example for your town leaders on why you need greater financial support for the library. It's not easy accommodating demand for increasing diversity in what you offer, but if you are successful in doing so, your public will love you and support you at budget time.

Complementing Other Community Resources

It's not uncommon for the public library to be a secondary library for school children. This can be an excellent partnership as long as the schools are not passing all their responsibilities to the public library. Considering the size of your budget, it is likely that you won't be able to afford to be both the school's and the public's library unless you receive the funding to do so. That doesn't mean you can't work to complement the school's resources. In fact, in most communities providing resources in support of homework assignments will be a critical role for the public library. It should be clear in your selection policy, however, that this is not the primary role of the public library and that your resources will *complement* and not *replace* a good school library.

Because ensuring that the children in your community get the after-school support they need for homework assignments, you may want to suggest that the school partner with you to provide students with the resources they need. Perhaps you could get on the school's "buy list" for textbooks so that you get copies of the major resources children need. Textbooks take up a lot of space so it might be possible to only house one copy of each. These can be placed on permanent reserve and made available after school hours and on weekends for those kids who find themselves on a school deadline with their backpacks in their lockers. Also, having these textbooks available at the public library will give parents a chance to see what their children are using now and what they will be learning next year.

You might also consciously avoid serious collection development in such areas as local history if there is a local historical society in town that makes its materials readily available to the public. You may also wish to state that you will not be a clearinghouse for, nor will you attempt to collect, materials which proselytize (or, seek to recruit one to a particular religion or cause).

Understanding what other resources are available in your community will help you make the most of the money you have for development. By complementing rather than overlapping these resources, you can spread your own dollar further and enhance the overall resources available to your citizens.

Collection Development and Your Community

In the end, your collection should be a true reflection of the community that uses it. No two public library collections are (or should be) alike just as no two towns are alike. Understanding the makeup of the community you serve is a critical component in your ability to develop a collection that will meet their needs.

Getting to know and understand the nature of your community comes in part from research, in part from discussion with staff and community members, and in part from plain old common sense. The research involves watching to see what circulates and what is being requested, in addition to reading local papers and being a participant in the community. Discussions with staff and patrons will help as much as anything in finding out what people are interested in. Common sense tells you that rural communities will have only slight interest in the problems of urban sprawl, while seacoast town libraries will have a special interest in books on ocean-related topics. Pretty easy, right? Now all you have to do is pick out which of the tens of thousands of books published each year will best reflect the nature of your community, and you've breezed through yet another year of collection development.

Giving Them What They Want

The frequent users in your libraries can be a mixed blessing. They are the ones who lead us to believe on the one hand that we're doing a great job, and on the other that we will *never* be able to do a good enough job to serve them fully. I've heard of one librarian (though I'm sure she is typical of others) who complained regularly that her library would be perfect if only she could keep the people out!

To a certain degree, I can sympathize with her frustrations. We all have ideals for library service that can be easily shattered by the realities of actual patrons. My ideal is that all patrons who come into the library leave with just the material or information they want. I think we all know the frustrations involved in measuring up to our own good press. What librarian, for example, doesn't love to see patrons lined up at the circulation desk to check out books? And what librarian doesn't cringe at the sight of patrons lined at the circulation desk requesting the *same* book?

In small libraries, buying duplicate titles to meet demand brings on an extra layer of frustration. Exceedingly small materials budgets mean that for every duplicate title we purchase, another desired title will go onto the wish list for next year (at best) or down the tubes altogether (at worst). It is important that you do all you can to serve your frequent users to the best of your ability, which is why you must swallow hard and buy an additional copy or two of a best seller and other popular items.

As hard as you try, however, you will probably never be able to keep up with the demand of the frequent users. Without infinite budgets and psychic abilities, there will always be times when a patron must leave your library with no more than a promise that you will call as soon as the materials she requested are available.

Here's where being entrepreneurial really pays off. If you understand your community well, you will know what kinds of books are going to be hot. Sure, you'll miss a particular title from time to time, but even if you're perfect, you'll never have the budget to satisfy every request every time. You can, however, satisfy your demanding patrons even when you don't have the particular title requested immediately available. This is where our readers' advisory role comes in. When a surprise (or not a surprise) best seller swells your reserve list, help your patrons discover your library's hidden treasures while they're waiting for their names to reach the top of the list. You have a huge investment in the collection, so look for ways to continuously exploit it. Displays of similar genres will move some of those older but still wonderful titles. Book lists that say, "If you like John Grisham you'll love … " make excellent bookmarks and give patrons a broader look at contemporary literature. Most patrons will welcome your recommendations and appreciate the fact that you've enhanced their reading repertoire. I believe most patrons count on us for that and it certainly is a very fulfilling part of our jobs.

Finally, don't miss a chance to be a good advocate for your library. If you find that consistently you are unable to stretch your materials budget to reasonably meet patron demand, let your patrons know that you are constrained by the budget. Those who use your library frequently can be your best advocates at budget time. Let them know that they can help by communicating their disappointment in your collection's limitations to those who fund you.

COLLECTING FOR THE INFREQUENT
OR POTENTIAL USER, NOT TO MENTION POSTERITY

The temptation is always to give *top* priority to the squeaky wheels. I've even heard some librarians advocate the continued purchase of duplicate copies of best sellers until the waiting list is completely eliminated. This would certainly make you popular with your regular users—there's no doubt about that. Is it, however, an ethical thing to do? Patrons who demand best sellers are not the only ones paying taxes. You have a wide range of constituents out there and, believe it or not, some of them *never* request a best seller. Some patrons come in only when they have to build a garage, fix their car, or read the employment ads in the newspaper of a neighboring large city. Can you readily serve these needs if the bulk of your materials budget is being spent to eliminate waiting lists?

The "Code of Ethics" endorsed by the American Library Association Council in 1981 states in the first sentence that "Librarians must provide the highest level of service through ... fair and equitable circulation and service policies" for their patrons. (See Appendix H—ALA Code of Ethics.) The philosophy of meeting high demand as a first priority says, in effect, that it is okay for some patrons to wait for materials through interlibrary loan, but it is not okay for another patron to wait for a best seller.

It may be old-fashioned, but I must confess to believing in well-rounded collections for public libraries. No community is one-dimensional; library collections that serve communities should not be one-dimensional either. Obviously, if your patrons love mysteries you will accommodate that love by providing a good collection of whodunits. And naturally, making this possible will mean less money for other areas.

More and more, we are also realizing the important archival role that public libraries play. I find it interesting and somewhat paradoxical that as we move deeper and deeper into the "digital age" the old role of public libraries as archives becomes more and more important. I am not saying that libraries should endeavor to become "book museums" but I am saying that part of what makes public libraries unique and, therefore, relevant in the Information Age is that we can provide the popular literary and historic record. As more and more information comes online (and offline) there is currently little thought or effort being put into archiving that material. I like to tell audiences who wonder why we need public libraries when we have the Internet that even though they can get lots of facts on the history of Virginia on the Internet, they can't, for example, get a *history* of Virginia on the Internet. Books are permanent—at least compared to digital information. Anyone who is looking for information published in its own time will most likely depend on a library—not the Internet—to find it. Small libraries can and should house the community's literary archive.

The trick in collection development is balance. The line has to be drawn somewhere between a collection that caters almost exclusively to heavy readers and one that reflects the diversity of the community it serves—both now and in the future. This is not an easy job. If collection development were a simple matter of anticipating and responding to popular interests, anyone could do it. The profession has long been aware that collection development just isn't that simple. It requires the careful thought and planning of a librarian who knows the community and understands the library's mission to serve *all* the people in it.

Your Library and Intellectual Freedom

What a time for public libraries! What an amazing time for small public libraries! With a link to the Internet and subscriptions to online databases, residents of small towns and villages can have the same access to information that is available to those living in the largest cities. Electronic resources have minimized the issues of space and, to some degree, the issues of cost. The advent of the Internet has been an incredible boon to those of us with limited budgets, space, and resources. Unfortunately, there is a downside. While the Internet provides the widest array of information imaginable, it is not discriminating as to the value, veracity or "appropriateness" of that material. This can pose some interesting and sometimes difficult problems for libraries.

THE INTERNET

While the opportunities for access have increased, so too has the widespread concern about just what can be accessed. There is no doubt about it, there are sites and images on the Internet that no responsible adult would want children to access. This presents an interesting dilemma for those of us who care deeply about children and what they are learning. While we wish to guide them in using this wonderful resource appropriately, we are confronted with very limited choices about effectively keeping them from material that truly is not appropriate.

Legislators (most of whom, I would argue, have little to no understanding about libraries and their mission) are quick to point to filtering technology as the answer.

The problem with this, as we well know, is that filters are ineffective in eliminating all "inappropriate" sites and images (how do they know?) and certainly they filter out a good deal of useful, not to mention constitutionally protected speech. So ... what *is* the answer? Librarians can and should hold fast to their traditional roles of actively guiding all patrons and particularly children in their use of the library. This is no more than what we've always done.

I am absolutely steadfast that the best filter is the human brain. Let's use ours and work with our children to teach them to use theirs. The fact is, we are in a new area with regard to information retrieval. I believe it is foolhardy to believe that children are at risk at our libraries and *particularly* at our libraries. Children do have and will continue to have access to online resources that are becoming increasingly ubiquitous. If not at our libraries, then at the local drug store, shopping mall, or at home—where parents, alas are not always at home. Increasingly, they will have access via palmtops, laptops, and who knows what new device on the horizon. Look at it this way—what could be more dangerous to a child than a street? If they cross a street without any education or guidance they could get hit by a car. This, of course, has the potential to be deadly. So what's the answer? Do we eliminate their access to streets altogether until they are adults or do we teach them how to cross the street safely? We have an important role to play in helping children become critical thinkers in the Information Age—to teach them to use the Internet safely.

We can help manage the use of the Internet in a way that maximizes its potential to be the valuable resource for learning that it is. Every library should have an Internet use policy that spells out how this resource is to be managed. In addition to spelling out your expectations for information access, this policy should also be used to manage its availability in the most equitable manner. For most libraries, demand exceeds the number of terminals available. In order that everyone who wishes to get online at the library has equal opportunity to do so, time limits should be set and regulations for sign-up spelled out. (See Appendix I—Internet Use Policy.)

THE PRINT COLLECTION

Protecting the rights of our patrons to unimpeded access to a wide variety of materials can be a difficult challenge in small libraries. The greatest threat to the integrity of our collections comes not from patrons but from ourselves if we agree to censor our terminals or our more traditional collections. We are constantly put in the position of deciding if we really want to include a particular item when we know or suspect it may cause a disturbance in our normally placid library.

It always surprises me a little when a review in the journals for our profession warns us about strong language or explicit sex. I've read tags at the end of a review such as "Some patrons may find this book upsetting" or "Librarians should take note of the graphic violence present in this novel." For me, making such warning statements in book reviews sends up a red flag immediately. The issue is not whether I want to be sure to avoid the item, but rather that I must now justify to myself why I am choosing *not* to purchase it, if that is indeed the case.

This kind of motive analysis is not a bad thing. In fact, it's necessary if we are to differentiate between selection and censorship. There seems to be no clear way to determine precensorship other than by examining (honestly) our own motives. What is our true intent when we opt not to purchase a potentially controversial item? If we are doing so because we feel it might raise objections or criticism, we must ask ourselves if this is a valid reason to suppress access to this concept or expression, and admit that we are engaging in censorship.

When it gets right down to it, the small-town librarian is seldom (if ever) challenged by the public for a controversial item she did *not* select. The ground is ripe for safe precensorship on the part of librarians and in the end, you are probably the only one who will know whether your library typifies true intellectual freedom or some sort of presanitized version of it. Librarians should not be the keepers of the public morals, however much we may think we would excel in that role.

Though it is fairly easy to take a strong stand in protecting our print collections for adults, what about placing questionable youth materials in the adult collection so that some impressionable younger children don't stumble on them accidentally? Our job is to promote intellectual freedom, not to provide barriers to it. As with the Internet, we do our children a greater service by working with them to help them be critical consumers of information, to learn what best meets their needs. If material by its reading or interest level belongs in the adult collection, put it there. If an item by its reading and interest level belongs in the children's room, put it there. The shelving of a questionable item should be based on the same objective criteria we use for all material. If parents are concerned about their children stumbling onto something "unsuitable," then they must monitor their children in the library; that job appropriately belongs to the parent.

AUDIOVISUAL MATERIALS

With various forms of media making huge inroads into libraries, old issues are being considered from new perspectives. This is certainly the case with censorship. Audiovisual materials can create new problems for some patrons. It's one thing to read about a torrid sexual encounter; it's another to watch it on television. Videos bring images out of the pages of books (and the minds of readers) onto the screen—the same issue, often, with the Internet. What used to be a private relationship between the reader and writer, with all images occurring solely in the mind, has become a more public relationship between all those involved with the video's production and the viewer. Now images are provided for you, and some of the privacy of the former relationship seems somehow violated.

Given this, there is likely to be much more sensitivity to your video (and even books-on-tape) collection than ever existed for the print media. Even though video and audio cassettes have become standard fare in libraries, they continue to be much bigger targets for censorship attempts than books. Because of this, you and your board must be prepared to articulate guidelines for audiovisual collection development and take a stand when and if that collection comes under fire.

There are several issues that will have to be addressed in your policy regarding audiovisual media. Some patrons may ask that you adhere to some sort of labeling system so they can be forewarned. Again, some serious soul-searching about the ethics of such a scheme is needed. If you plan to follow the Library Bill of Rights, you are already aware that labeling is unacceptable. You are on sound ground to treat these materials as you do any in the collection and require that patrons make their own (and their own children's) decisions about what they wish to watch or hear. It's as easy to turn off a television as it is to close a book.

In truth, most patrons will be able to ascertain from the jacket, title and description of a video if it is likely to offend them or their children. If you receive complaints about a video or book-on-tape, it will probably be because the patron feels it is not suitable for the public in general. This sort of subjective judgment on the part of a patron is just the thing we do not tolerate for our print collection. If videos and all other materials are originally selected for good reasons, those haven't changed, and the material should be allowed to remain in the collection as originally shelved.

PROTECTING INTELLECTUAL FREEDOM: THE WRITTEN SELECTION POLICY

It seems probable that one reason small libraries receive little pressure from outside groups and individuals to censor library materials is because many librarians tend to have already censored their acquisitions. Most small-library collections are, in fact, pretty tame. In spite of that, there usually comes a time in the life of every librarian when a patron or group suggests, recommends, urges or demands that you remove, label or reshelve an item in your library. This is your chance to make a truly meaningful stand in favor of intellectual freedom. You can almost always do this with a minimum of confrontation if you have done your homework in advance. Develop a selection policy that includes your library's position on censorship as well as a statement that the library supports the American Library Association's Bill of Rights (which you have appended to your policy—see Appendix G).

One very effective tool in warding off serious attempts to proscribe materials in the library is a "Patron Request Form for Reconsideration of a Work" (see Appendix J—Patron Request for Reconsideration). A carefully considered and detailed form will probably daunt all but the most fanatical would-be censors. It will strongly imply that you take the issue seriously but that you will not be easily swayed to remove or reshelve materials.

Be prepared, however, for the eventuality that a patron or group will fill out the form in full and expect you to take further action. Your selection policy should outline clearly the procedure for removal or reshelving of books. After the form has been filled out, the next step is generally a meeting between the person complaining, you and the board of trustees. It's important that the trustees who have helped formulate your selection policy be familiar with it and ready to defend it.

CENSORSHIP AND PUBLICITY

If the problem is still not resolved after an open board meeting, and you feel that the situation might escalate, it is probably time for you to inform the press, the state library and your state's intellectual freedom committee.

I know of one librarian who tried desperately to keep a censorship attempt at her library under wraps. A small but assertive group of parents from a fundamentalist church were very concerned about some of the young adult novels available at the library. This group went through the entire complaint procedure and was demanding that the books be removed. After much discussion with the library's board of trustees, the group reached a compromise position requesting that the books be reshelved in the adult collection.

The librarian felt that if word got out, other groups would try their hands at censorship. She knew a terrible precedent was being set. In her frustration over the situation, the librarian finally confided in a favorite patron who became outraged. The next day the librarian received a call from the local paper, and an article about the incident was published. Before long, the library was receiving complaints from all quarters—not to request further reshelving or removal of other books, but voices of outrage that one small fundamentalist group could circumvent the public library's policy.

What ensued was a public hearing where it was clear that the public supported neither the views of this group nor the notion that books in the public library should be removed or reshelved simply because one group finds them offensive. I'm happy to report that the books are back in the young adult room and as far as I know, that group has never questioned the library's collection since.

The issue of publicity becomes a little trickier with regard to the Internet and filtering. Your public may not understand filtering technology very well and they are likely to see it as an obvious solution—with no downside. We must work hard to educate our communities about what is gained and what is lost when we use filters. It has been my experience that when I discuss the nature of filters in an objective, nonemotional way, most patrons agree that the gain is not worth the loss. It takes courage to stand up for unfettered access—some will want to paint you as a person who doesn't care about children, in league with pornographers. It's very important to try to stay objective and work to educate your public. You will be surprised how understanding they can be.

An important thing to remember is that you have a lot of support out there; don't hesitate to use it. The history of censorship attempts in libraries shows that the general public is not usually too sympathetic toward censorship, so it is likely that once the community is aware that there is a threat to the collection, they will support you and the library's policy.

Gifts

The problem of waste disposal being what it is today, I for one have begun to look a gift horse in the mouth when it comes to library donations. Surely there is no librarian who's been in practice for more than a year or so who hasn't been the recipient of dear departed Aunt Mildred's (fill in the name of your choosing) collection of childhood favorites. Old and moldy, these gems are deposited without guilt on the library's doorstep that just happens to be centrally located. Not only is the library drop-off free (as opposed to the county dump), the "gift" can be taken as a tax write-off as well.

To be a little more fair and a lot less cynical, there are many well-meaning folks out there who honestly believe that any book is a good book. It is to our own discredit that there are others who feel that *anything* is good enough for the town library. Because most of these people are truly well-meaning, the acceptance of gifts can be a touchy area indeed; that's why a written statement in the collection policy pertaining to gifts is so important.

A well-written, specific policy can save you and your staff the embarrassment of ever having to tell Aunt Mildred's heirs that her books stink (both literally and figuratively). The policy should specifically state that the same objective criteria used for the purchase of new books will be applied to the acceptance of gift books. It should state that books included in the collection must be in excellent condition and, in most cases, up to date. The policy should state clearly what isn't acceptable; reference books over five years old or textbooks, for example.

SELLING GIFT BOOKS

Just because a particular book isn't good enough for your collection, however, doesn't mean it doesn't have value for your library. Library book sales are common, sound and prudent endeavors that have the double benefit of raising extra money and giving old books one more chance before making that fateful trip to the dump. Whether it's the library's staff or the Friends of the Library who manage the book sale, it will be helpful to include in the gift policy a statement that makes it clear that the librarian reserves the right to accept a book for inclusion in the collection, to put the book in a book sale, or to reject the gift. To make final rejection easier, it would be wise to include a list of what is not acceptable for the book sale as well. This might include such items as textbooks, encyclopedia sets over 15 years old, and *Reader's Digest* condensed books. You can provide your patrons with a "thank you," a gift receipt, and a short description of your gift acceptance policy in one simple handout. (See Appendix K—Sample Gift Acknowledgement/Receipt.)

The beauty of a written policy is that it can take the sting out of rejection for both you and the donor. Policies are by nature impersonal; they are developed outside of and prior to the particular situation you now face. You will be armed with objective criteria that have nothing to do with Aunt Mildred personally but with the books that are outside your selection parameters and won't move at the book sale.

ENCOURAGING GIFTS

There are, of course, those gifts you wish to encourage. Many libraries and Friends groups have had success in launching "Buy a Book for the Library" campaigns. These often involve honoring someone you care about, be it as a memorial or as a birthday present. When successful, these campaigns can really help enhance a book collection, but again, there are some issues here that should be examined before beginning such a campaign.

First of all, make sure that if you have a "Buy a Book for the Library" campaign, you do what is necessary to retain control of collection development. To keep control, you should require that the actual purchasing of the book be left to you or your staff. You can accept title and subject suggestions, of course, but the final decision should remain up to the librarian. If you allow just any book to be given in memory or honor of someone, you are likely to get titles you don't need, or (even worse) you could get Aunt Mildred's books with the added request that bookplates be put in them in her memory.

Perhaps the most important issue to address is the success of the campaign itself and where that might eventually lead. Because money for books and other materials in the library's collection must come from the library's budget, it should be clear from the beginning that any money raised will be used just to *expand* and *augment* the collection. Be sure you're clear that it will not be used *in place of* a standard materials budget. Ironically, the more successful you are in raising money for your library, the more the town government is likely to expect it of you. If you are put in the position of having to raise money for the existence of an adequate collection your library's future well-being will be put in jeopardy and change your job description radically. Engaging in projects to enhance the collection is truly important; just make sure these projects don't become *too* important.

Stretching the Materials Budget

Once you and your trustees have done everything possible to provide the library with a good operating budget, there are ways to make that budget go a little further. Librarians are nothing if not creative. By putting that creative instinct together with the ever-present desire for more purchasing power, you can come up with a variety of ways to get more book for the buck.

There are four basic ways to stretch the materials budget. You can increase it through gifts (both monetary and material), you can increase the purchasing power of the money you do have, you can find ways to share, and you can employ policies and procedures that generate the best turnover rates possible for your most popular items.

HIGH TURNOVER

Best sellers are money monsters. Our most loyal patrons are often those who want the best sellers—and they want them *now!* Meeting this demand can take a real toll on an already too-small materials budget because you are forced to buy multiple copies of a title that will be passé in a year. Not meeting this demand takes a real toll on the quality of customer service you are able to provide. Many libraries across the country have found effective ways to meet this high demand and at a lower (though never cheap) cost.

One effective method is to limit the loan period on best sellers. You may want to develop a policy that states that titles which have been requested by five or more patrons will trigger a special loan period of seven days until that item is no longer in such high demand. If you typically loan materials for three weeks, this will reduce your length of time a patron will have to wait for a reserve by up to two-thirds. This is a very attractive reason to begin such a policy. Initially, your best-seller readers will likely protest at having a shorter period of time to read the book. My experience tells me that typical best-seller readers are fast readers and they often check out many books at a time. Having a shorter term in which to read a hot item will force them, perhaps, to take out fewer books, but it will certainly force them to read the high-demand items first. You can add to the overall acceptance of a new and shorter loan period by ordering duplicate titles that might be labeled "Book Express." These duplicate best-selling titles would not be available for reserve, but the upside is that it is likely that a hot item or two would be on the shelves for the new-books browser.

Shorter loan periods for videos are pretty common and they serve the same purpose: they allow more people to enjoy a high-demand item sooner than if they had to wait two or three weeks for each preceding patron to finish with it. In the end, most libraries who use reduced loan periods will tell you that the patrons like getting reserves sooner, and that in the end the library buys far fewer multiple copies—that means more money for more variety in the collection.

BORROWING FROM PATRONS

Raising additional funds for books and materials has been done successfully by many libraries and Friends groups. The ways to do this are limited only by your collective imaginations.

In addition to a "Give a Book to the Library" campaign, you can encourage the giving of other books by your community, which will help you meet a high demand at a low cost to your materials budget. Because best sellers are both costly and fleeting (in terms of sustained high interest) you might be successful in promoting a "Loan a Book to the Library" campaign. The idea here is to tap into those people who actually *buy* books either at bookstores or through book clubs. People who want books hot off the press will probably read them right away. Many would probably feel good about sharing those books with others via the public library. Why not publish a weekly list of books that have waiting lists along with an appeal to borrow them. The owners could be promised that when the demand subsides, the books will be returned. Sure they'll be a little worn and they will have a library stamp or two, but you'll be affording people a wonderful opportunity to make a meaningful contribution to the library without ever opening their pocketbooks.

BEING A SMART CONSUMER

You can always increase the purchasing power of your budget simply by being a smart consumer. When was the last time you called three or four vendors to let them know you were shopping around for the best discount available? Try it sometime, and be sure to let the distributors know that you will share the information. You might be able to get the discount you are currently receiving up a point or two. Similarly, you should be sure to contact your state library to see if there is a buying cooperative you could join and if so, compare the discount the cooperative is getting with your own. Be sure when you are doing comparison shopping that you take into account any variable discounts, which can be quite low for paperbacks and children's books. A discount of 40 percent on everything might save you a lot more than a discount that is 43 percent for hardbacks but only 10 percent for children's books and paperbacks.

Buying through jobbers is, of course, the most expedient method of getting books and other library materials but it is not always the cheapest. Don't throw out those clearinghouse catalogs that turn up regularly in the mail. You should keep a wish list of materials that don't make it in the first round of buying or that are just a little too high priced for you to justify (art books and "coffee table" books for example). Spend a day or two each year poring over clearinghouse catalogs and comparing the items offered with your wish list; you are likely to find some wonderful (and inexpensive) surprises.

SHARING

Sharing is another way to stretch the budget, and sharing is really what libraries are all about. Because the concept is central to our existence, it really is no wonder that librarians are willing to share so freely among themselves. Use this spirit to prevail upon larger libraries in your area (public or academic) to give you their year-old (or even two-year-old) editions of basic reference works when they update them.

You will be surprised at how accommodating your colleagues in larger libraries can be. Many small libraries can function perfectly well with a two- to three-year-old edition of a periodicals directory or directory of associations for example. While the information will be dated to some extent (as with prices, for example) most addresses and phone numbers, along with names, will still be valid. It's important, of course, that you do your best to provide the most current information available, but reference materials that are just a couple of years old are generally still useful for small libraries.

Sharing can also extend beyond the receipt of secondhand items. If your library belongs to an areawide consortium, perhaps you could consider dividing up the purchase of important but expensive reference works so that lesser-used titles aren't duplicated among you. This wouldn't work well, of course, for those items patrons typically use themselves (like the "Value Line") or those that have lengthy entries (such as encyclopedias). For directories, special dictionaries and other quick reference works, however, you can save a lot of money by becoming involved in this kind of networking. Think about it; you can make a lot of long-distance calls to a neighboring library and pay for a lot of faxes before you'd spend the $400 that a publications directory might cost.

Because many of the traditional resources are now available online, you should work with other libraries in your area to form a cooperative for these subscriptions as well. Consider other types of libraries as well as other regional public libraries. Your hospital may already subscribe to medical databases that can be shared, even at a cost. Similarly, local college and university libraries usually have a significant investment in online resources. Contact the vendors of online resources and find out how and if they can work with you to make these products more widely available and affordable in your area. You will need to negotiate a licensing agreement, though, which will likely be costly. In the long run, these kinds of partnerships with other libraries and entities are likely to save you money and enhance the materials available to your patrons.

Another kind of network sharing might work well to expand the videos you are able to offer without a corresponding increase in this line item. Because video collections are usually fairly small in small libraries, and because patrons go through videos much more quickly than they do books, you might want to work out an exchange program with other area libraries with similar sized video collections. After some of your more popular titles have made the rounds among all the interested patrons (twice!), you might want to swap these straight across with another library for the same number of different videos. An across the board exchange will benefit everyone, and if the trade is "for keeps" (at least until you're ready to trade again with another library), this plan need not be complicated or take up much time.

When you are finding ways to stretch the materials budget you'll have to keep in mind the time and effort you and your staff spend, and weigh that against the benefits. Without making money-stretching your life's work, you should be able to come up with several ways to enhance your collection within the constraints of your operating budget.

Weeding the Collection

I believe that weeding requires more professional judgment and serious thought than selection. When you remove older titles from your collection, you may well be removing access to a particular title permanently. Thanks to changes in the 1986 tax laws that penalize publishers' inventories, books go out of print much more quickly than ever before. This means that when you remove an older title from your collection, you may not be able to retrieve it again, even through interlibrary loan. This doesn't mean that you shouldn't weed, however, or even that you shouldn't weed assiduously. It's just that you should be as particular about what is allowed to stay in the collection as you are about what will go into it in the first place, and you should think hard about the potential use it may have. Bottom line, public libraries do have a responsibility to provide the depth in their collections that bookstores do not, but we're not archives and our job is to provide materials that will be relevant and used. Well-weeded collections see higher circulation. Why make your patrons wade through tons of junk to come up with a gem? And, more importantly, after all we do to tout our services and fine collections, why would we want patrons to find dirty, out-of-date materials of questionable value on our shelves?

MAINTAINING CREDIBILITY

Before determining whether a particular item should remain in the library's collection, perhaps the most important idea to repudiate is that *anything* on a subject is better than nothing at all. Wrong, wrong, wrong! Out of date and erroneous information is *not* better than nothing at all. Implicit in the obligation to provide our patrons with information, it seems to me, is to provide them with *reliable* information, at least insofar as that can be determined. Thanks to the Internet and other online resources, it may not be necessary at all to have print materials in some subjects—especially those subjects that change rapidly and are more information-oriented than they are oriented to analysis and context.

If you want to establish credibility as a resource center, you must be sure that you respond to changes in different fields of knowledge by getting rid of that which has been superseded, and replacing it. Some librarians look at the circulation history of an item as justification in itself for keeping it. What a heavy circulation record tells *them* about a 1960 physics book is that it's still popular. What it tells *me* is that the field of physics is still popular, so I'd better get rid of the antique and get a new book (perhaps two!) on the subject.

What if you can't find or afford a good, up-to-date book in a particular area? Shouldn't you keep the old book until you're able to replace it? Not if you're interested in maintaining the integrity of your collection. Again, online resources may well supplant the need to have print materials in certain areas—or at least they may allow you to have fewer. What is on your shelves, in any case, must be works that contain good, accurate information, unless they are historical materials that are kept to provide insight into the perspectives and thinking of a particular period of time. Imagine this scenario. There's a man in your community who hasn't been in a library since high school. If asked, he would tell you that libraries are boring, stodgy and perhaps slightly elitist. He would rank the library's importance in the community somewhere just below heating the local pool, if he thought about it at all—which he never does.

One day this man decides to make a big leap and start his own business from his home. He needs to know what's new in office equipment. It sticks in his mind somewhere that libraries have information on all kinds of things (he's heard the radio public service messages and noticed the library's column in the newspaper from time to time). He hardly remembers how to use the library but decides to give it a go. He feels uncomfortable asking for help, so he manages on his own to find the section on business machines where the only book he finds is a 1962 title extolling the virtues of the newfangled electric typewriter.

What is he likely to think of your library now? Sure, you've got great books on computers in another section of the library and you could have helped him consult *Consumer Reports*. This man, however, like many (most?) patrons, didn't ask for help. He found what he thought was the extent of your collection in his area of interest. Now he has one more adjective to add to his list about the library: worthless. All this could have been prevented by having either up-to-date information in the area of business equipment, or nothing—at least that might have prompted him to ask. The worst that could have happened, did. He found ridiculously out-of-date information that confirmed all his worst instincts about libraries.

LOOKING GOOD

Once you've become braver about creating holes in the collection (you can keep wish lists and work to fill them; that's what collection development is all about), you have other criteria to use in judging the usefulness of a particular item. Condition of a book is another important element in determining whether you want to keep an item in the collection. If a book is dirty, torn or just plain ugly, make a note of it and find out if you can get a new copy to replace it. You might even consider a quality paperback in favor of a worn-out hardback copy. If the book is out of print, consider sending it off to the binders.

THE CLASSICS

When it comes to classics, even the most active of weeders has a difficult time. Can you really consider throwing out *Romeo and Juliet* even though it hasn't circulated since 1967? What about that gorgeous leather-bound set of James Fenimore Cooper's complete works? (They were given in 1906 and have gone out, on average, three times a year since then.) How about the novels of Charles Dickens? They are classics, after all, even if no one seems to read them. Do not despair; we can keep our classics and perhaps get our patrons to read them, too.

A little thought and a touch of marketing can give new life to your classics. First of all, get rid of the sets. They might look good with tweed and pipes, but they obviously aren't looking too good to your patrons. In my own (very personal and subjective) opinion, you can forget the Cooper altogether. However, if you feel there is hope for his works in your library, get out *Books in Print* and find out who publishes his works in quality paperback. The same goes for Thackeray and others of similar interest. If these books aren't being subjected to heavy circulation you don't need those sturdy leather bindings anyway. Sell them in your book sale. Quality paperbacks are inexpensive (you may be able to pay for them from the sale of those sets) and they are much more appealing to popular audiences. Once you get spiffy new copies, announce it to your world by putting up a "Rediscover the Classics" display. You'll be astonished at the results.

As for the major authors and playwrights, such as Shakespeare, you can clean up your collection by getting rid of most of the lesser known or less popular individual titles and replacing the "big" ones with quality paperbacks. To cover the broad range of a writer's works you can get by nicely by adding one or two well reviewed "complete works" (making sure that the print is not too small). With these sorts of collections, you will be sure that the occasional patron looking for minor works of major writers will find them in your library.

IMPROVING ACCESS AND CIRCULATION

Knowing that you will be improving access and browsability by weeding, you will feel better about setting an arbitrary circulation requirement on books for them to earn their shelf space. A good rule of thumb for most books would be to require that they each have circulated at least once in the last five years in order to be kept. Of course, this will always have to be balanced with the book's intrinsic importance to the collection as a whole and the book's probable "in-house" use which might not be reflected on the circulation record. These decisions require the good judgment of you and your staff. You must make the decisions based on the same knowledge of your community and the various fields of information that you apply to book selection.

Beyond the Library Walls

No matter how well you have developed the collection, no matter how diverse and responsive it is to your community, you will have to go beyond your own library's walls from time to time in order to meet the needs of your patrons. Certainly, providing access to the Internet and other online resources expands this opportunity dramatically. But not everything is online of course. Because libraries are by nature cooperative, and librarians by nature resourceful, it is possible for patrons to enter their own library and receive, in the end, materials from another library, materials and information found through database searching, or referral to the appropriate agency.

Interlibrary Loan

Our best-kept secret is the fact that if we don't have a book on our shelves, we can get it from another library. I can't think of any service the library provides that gets us more kudos and appreciation than our willingness to find a book—no matter how obscure, no matter when published—and borrow it from another library. The simple idea of sharing resources has become a staple of library service. Interlibrary loan has enabled libraries across the country to expand the limits of their collections immeasurably. The provision of this service may indeed net the local library more praise and grateful response than anything else we provide. How many times have we all had patrons give heartfelt thanks for our having "gone to so much trouble."

Interlibrary loan is a wonderful service, and thanks to automated online union catalogs, it's a service that is being delivered more rapidly and more efficiently. Small libraries especially benefit by being able to offer this service, making access to a wide variety of information and materials a reality.

EXAMINING THE COSTS

As terrific as interlibrary loan is, however, it does have some drawbacks that warrant attention when policy and procedures for its use are being developed. The most obvious drawback is, of course, cost. While it may be more expensive to buy a book than to borrow it, borrowing should not be looked upon as a cheap alternative. Interlibrary loan takes staff time from both your library and the lending library. Interlibrary loan systems depending on the United States mail face the additional cost of postage, which continues to rise.

The other drawback to interlibrary loan is waiting time. Even if you have next-day service, that doesn't help the patron who comes in three hours before an interview to look at your résumé handbooks (and use one of your computers, too!). Without making any subjective judgments about this patron's timing, it's clear to all of us that patrons often need the information they seek *now*.

NEGOTIATING THE REQUEST

So, am I saying that interlibrary loan really isn't that great after all? Certainly not. I am saying, however, that there are costs (sometimes significant) attached, and it's a good idea to be aware of them to help hold the line as well as you can. First, it makes sense to treat interlibrary loan requests as you do reference requests. Take some time to talk with the patron to be sure that what he is asking for is *really* what he wants. Just because a patron asks for a book called *The ABCs of Golfing* doesn't mean that he wouldn't be just as happy (or happier) with another book you have available on golfing that is up to date and well reviewed. In fact, any good book on how to golf might be acceptable, but the *ABC* book was the only one he knew about. It's amazing how well you can satisfy most patrons with a small, well-developed collection. Be sure your own resources have been exhausted before sending for someone else's. Not only will you save money, but you will have served your patron better by having been more expedient.

MAKING THE MOST OF THE SYSTEM

If you do depend a good deal on interlibrary loan you should keep track not only of the number of requests you make but also the kinds. If you find you are ordering the same title or subject more than twice a year, you will be doing both the budget and your patrons a favor by ordering the book as a permanent addition to the collection.

Finally, if you are part of a state or regional system, you can greatly facilitate the efficiency of that system by becoming well versed in the procedures you are asked to follow. This may seem a small thing, but large systems work best (and cheapest) if everyone using them follows a standard set of procedures. If you delegate interlibrary loan, be sure the person responsible is sensitive to both the benefits and the drawbacks so that the service you offer can be as efficient as possible.

Online Resources

The fact that information is now often accessible by computer is truly exciting (and perhaps a little scary and overwhelming as well). For small libraries, it means that the day has come when regardless of size or geographic location we can offer the same access to information that the largest city libraries can. Electronic access to information is surely a great equalizer in terms of a library's ability to serve its patrons.

Despite the tremendous potential these resources have to maximize our services, there are costs involved—money, space, and time. It's important that we make the case for these. The money needed for the infrastructure—wiring, hardware, and furnishings—may well be available through local and national grants. You can make a very compelling case for the library's role in closing the digital divide and well you should. The Bill and Melinda Gates Foundation has become the new "Carnegie" in terms of their tremendous financial support for the development of this infrastructure in libraries. It is very likely that you have Gates computers right now. Often, local foundations are most willing to build on these gifts and it's important to leave no stone unturned in finding all the financial support you can for the development and growth of your online infrastructure.

The financial costs don't stop with the installation of public computer stations, however. Telecommunication costs will rise as your library becomes more "wired" and as opportunities to raise the speed of your network increase. Though we have, in recent years, received some financial relief from federal programs like "e-rate" funds, those funds are always at risk and at the whim of legislators who, recently, have supported holding them hostage in exchange for filtering requirements. It's important that we consider the costs of telecommunication charges as we build our electronic access.

One of the big myths that we've seen dispelled is that electronic information will free up much needed space in your library because it will enable you to acquire fewer print resources. Indeed, there will be some exchange, but what we are really finding is that online information expands our ability to provide information services without, in large part, supplanting print resources. Not only that, but computer stations take up space—lots of space! So, as you are building this new infrastructure for your library, be sure to be keeping those who fund you aware of all the true costs—including the price you pay in terms of floor space.

Finally, all the grants in the world probably won't make up for the costs of tremendously increased demands on our staff time. The day may come when our public knows how to effectively use electronic resources as they do our print resources. But even then, the value that libraries offer to their users will still be librarian assistance and mediation. As information access continues to grow and become more complex, our role as information navigators will also increase. These new and increasing demands take much more staff time than more traditional services have and, in addition, put much more importance on staff training. We will not be able to maximize electronic resources for our patrons if we, ourselves, are not well trained and do not remain up to date on what's out there and how to best make use of it. All of this is costly—and darn well worth it!

Cost Versus Benefit

Libraries have a new, or perhaps more appropriately, a *renewed* role in ensuring that members of their community have all the tools they need to learn, grow, and fully participate in the Information Age. Public libraries have a long and proud history of ensuring that all people, regardless of means, background, age, or point of view have access to the information they need for lifelong learning and intellectual stimulation and growth. Public libraries are the most democratic of all institutions because they offer—for free!—equal opportunity access to the widest array of materials possible.

Now, with the Internet, the stakes have become even higher. The "Digital Divide" continues to widen between those who can afford access to online resources and those who can't. In keeping with over 200 years of tradition, the public library is making it possible for even the poorest among us to participate in this information revolution. In the end, it is critical for us to make the case for the funding and support necessary to protect the free and unfettered flow of information in all its formats, both present and future. While it is nothing new, librarians must ensure that those who fund us understand the vital issues—what it will cost to keep libraries viable institutions in the community, and, more importantly, why it matters to do so.

In speaking to an audience at the New York Public Library in 1997, Toni Morrison said this of libraries:

> Access to knowledge is the superb, the supreme act of truly great civilizations. Of all the institutions that purport to do this, free libraries stand virtually alone in accomplishing this mission. No committee decides who may enter, no crisis of body or spirit must accompany the entrant. No tuition is charged, no oath sworn, no visa demanded. Of the monuments humans build for themselves, very few say "touch me, use me, my hush is not indifference, my space is not barrier. if I inspire awe, it is because I am in awe of you and the possibilities that dwell in you."

If directors of small libraries don't look to the future with the understanding that we are in the midst of great change, our patrons will be at a decided disadvantage. We must ensure that all people in this country, whether living in a major metropolitan area or in a remote, rural corner, have equal access to information. In the end, this can only happen if they are provided with equal means. The cost of this access remains a public responsibility.

For all of us in small libraries who shape the services to our communities, providing equal access to information may be our biggest challenge. It is a challenge that I believe will be well met. Directing a small library, turning it from a quaint reading room into a resource center that performs a vital function in the community, is not a job for the faint of heart—and it is not a job to think about *tomorrow*.

FOUR

The Library Building

Who among us has not been asked, "Will we really need libraries in the future when we can get all the information we need on the Internet?" Even though we have entered what is often referred to as the "Information Age," all of us are fielding more and more questions about the relevancy of the library in the digital age. It is easy to come up with answers about the importance of libraries in closing the digital divide. Most people can readily understand the library role in equalizing access to electronic, online information ... *today*. But, do we honestly believe that the time won't come when access to the Internet is nearly universal?

Telecommunication advances are bringing faster speeds at lower prices. Steps have already taken place to integrate Internet access with television. Hardware for access is growing beyond desktop computers to include not only television sets, but hand-held devices, and all of these continue to offer more power at less cost. While it is well known that access to the Internet is growing faster for white, middle-class Americans than for Americans of color, overall access *is* increasing—rapidly. It is true that public libraries have an absolutely vital role to play as we transition into a world where access to online information changes our lives forever, especially in its role as an equalizer between the haves and have-nots (which is a role that public libraries have always played). But, when we look around at how fast the transition is taking place, it really isn't that hard to imagine a future time (and I would argue, near future) when access to online information becomes ubiquitous—when the digital divide closes significantly if not completely.

This brings us back to the original question. If we can imagine a day in the not too distant future when most citizens have access to online information, will we really need library buildings? Or so many of them? Or of a significant size? My answer is, absolutely! Our communities need libraries now and for the future, perhaps, more than ever before and of sufficient size and numbers that they can truly fulfill their historic and increasingly important role of community learning center. For one thing, the print world does not seem to be diminished at all by burgeoning technological resources. Look at your desk right now—is it evidence of a paperless society? In fact, more books are published each year than in the year before. If you don't believe me, visit your local Barnes and Noble next time you get a chance. Or better yet, take a look at what's going on in your own library.

Libraries have always played a critical role in the community not just because of the books on the shelf, but because they offer a unique opportunity for people of all ages, from all walks of life to get the materials and learning resources they need in an interactive way. With assistance from library staff, and through programs, browsing, and serendipity, patrons have come into our libraries and have received a "human" learning experience. In addition, they have counted on us for a wider variety of materials than one would ever find in a bookstore. Try finding a ten-year-old seminal work in a specialized subject area at your local bookstore.

In addition to standing as important community centers (unique in that they serve everyone with expert assistance freely and without regard to means, age, or interest), public libraries have always played and continue to play a key archival role in amassing and making perpetually available the record of the human experience. It's an awesome and important role. Who besides libraries are keeping this heritage and making it readily available, thus providing context for all other current and future learning and understanding?

The plain fact of the matter is that library buildings are needed now to provide not only traditional services, but support technological information access and be prepared for as yet unknown services in the future. That we capture all the learning resources we can and make them publicly available through the library is more important in the Information Age than at any other time in our past. Libraries have always been the literacy safety net in their communities. Beginning with babies and throughout life, the library is there to provide the resources, encouragement, and joy in lifelong learning. Today literacy in its broadest sense (including technological literacy and the ability to understand and use information well) is job number one. In today's world with diminishing opportunities to prosper by work of one's hands, the ability to read and to use information technology effectively is critical to life success. Now, as in the past, libraries stand out as the people's university.

What *has* changed in recent years is not the relevancy of our library buildings but the importance of those buildings in bringing a much larger and growing array of resources together with the people who need them and the staff who can maximize their value to patrons. Library buildings now take center stage in our Information Age. They have become truly our temples of lifelong learning. Library buildings need to be readily accessible to all our community members, they must be large enough to accommodate traditional as well as emerging resources, and they must allow for interaction between library staff and patrons, for interaction between one patron and another, and for group learning. If libraries are to succeed in building community, they must be housed in buildings that will help all of us achieve that goal.

A Fresh Look—The Aesthetics

When was the last time you really took a good look at your library building? It is so easy to get mired in the daily routine and function of the library that after a time most of us don't even notice the building anymore.

As long as it's relatively warm in the winter and cool in the summer; as long as a toilet doesn't need plunging (ten minutes after the custodian leaves); and as long as you can still squeeze one more book onto the shelf—it's pretty easy to take the building for granted.

Try an experiment. Take time out to walk past and then into the library with your eyes wide open. Try to see your library as your patrons do. Does it stand out on the street? Can you tell it's a library at a glance? Do you feel welcomed on entering? Once you are inside, can you tell where you are? Does this look like an inviting place to read, study, complete a project, use the computers, and check out books?

You might surprise yourself when you take a good, objective look at your library. You may notice that the walls are dingy and the lighting poor. You might realize that a newcomer would never figure out that those book stacks in the lobby contain the newly cataloged arrivals. And, if someone is confused, he will have trouble locating a reference librarian or a circulation clerk. You might even admit (if you've been avoiding it) that the place is just too crowded.

It's a safe bet that most of us did not get into the library biz to think about buildings, but the truth is, your building has a direct impact on the service you provide.

There's no getting around it—facility maintenance and management is an important part of the library director's responsibility. Working with your facility so that it fully supports your library service can actually be creative and fun, believe it or not.

The Exterior

YOUR FIRST IMPRESSION

The library building can and should be a source of civic pride. If it is to be the temple of learning that it is to so many of our patrons, it should look like it. OK, so maybe you don't have the Taj Mahal, but regardless of architecture or age you can and should work hard to make the library stand out in a positive way. Philosophically, I think the library building conveys a strong message about its place of importance in the civic scheme of things. In a perfect world, every library in every town would be the hallmark piece of architecture—in some towns, they are! In the meantime, however, we can ensure a pride of place by providing excellent landscaping and always keeping the exterior looking its best.

The front of your building conveys the first impression people have of your service. Take a good look. What you should see is a building in excellent repair. It should have grounds that are pleasant and well kept; there should be a sign you can't miss that tells you the name of the library and its hours of operation. And, of course, you should be able to see clearly how you get in—even if you are in a wheelchair, on crutches, or pushing a baby stroller.

MAINTENANCE

Keeping the exterior of the library in good repair is an ongoing project. The amount of time it takes depends on the building itself. If some sadist in the past designed a lovely clapboard façade, you will probably have to paint on a regular basis—something to keep in mind if you are planning new construction. On the other hand, a stone or brick building will require a lot less maintenance. Still, window casings may have to be painted periodically and window screens and storm windows should be in good repair.

Even if you can't actually see it, don't forget the roof. It will save you money and aggravation in the long run if you mark your calendar every spring with a reminder to call your local roofing company. For a reasonable fee, they will check the integrity of your roof and clean out the gutters. If repairs are necessary, it's best to find out about it *before* there is a leak onto the book stacks. Routine maintenance is your best defense against more costly repairs later.

THE GROUNDS

Having beautiful grounds is not a just a matter of conceit—a beautiful yard helps to give the library high visibility and can also make your library feel like a more welcoming and pleasant place. Without spending a lot of money, you can do little things that can make all the difference in your library's exterior image.

First and foremost, the grounds should be kept clean and neat at all times. This means that rubbish is always picked up, the lawn is mowed and the hedges clipped. If you have overgrown bushes or trees climbing up the front (and blocking light to the inside) you should consider trimming them back or removing them and replacing them with low, flowering shrubs.

Once you have assured yourself that the basics of grounds care have been handled, you might consider calling in the local garden club to see if they would be interested in taking on the library as a summer project. Here's a good chance for both of you to get better exposure. You will benefit by free landscape design and care, while the garden club will benefit by the publicity they receive for creating a beautiful garden for one of the most prestigious buildings in town—the public library.

You can increase the welcoming spirit as well by including benches in your landscape design. Do you really want people on the library lawn? Sure, why not? It's the public's library, and think how appealing it will be for people to spend their lunch hours reading on the library lawn and enjoying a nice summer breeze. Providing a place for people to sit is a surefire way to say welcome.

Finally, be sure that you have a sign right out in front where everyone, even those people whipping past in their cars, can see it. This is not the place to be tastefully discreet. Tasteful, yes, discreet, no. With bold letters, state your library's name and list the hours you are open. It might not be a bad idea to include a statement such as "The Public Is Welcome" or "Founded in 1866 for All the People of Centerville."

ACCESS FOR THE DISABLED

I believe that people with disabilities are the library's *invisible* underserved constituency; we typically don't do a very good job at all in serving them. If you don't believe me, take a look around your own library. How many patrons do you see using wheelchairs or walkers ... probably not many. In all probability, this isn't because there aren't many in your community who are disabled, but rather that they can't easily use the library so they don't come. Now imagine how many people there are with disabilities that you can't see—those with sight or hearing impairment, or those with respiratory challenges.

There are, of course, minimum standards for access to public buildings for those people who have disabilities. Providing access has been high on the list of priorities for most libraries. You might want to put together a special task force including representation from your trustees, your staff, the local assistive-living facility, a patron with disabilities, and a member from your town's human resource department. Have this task force take a good look at your library and the equipment inside to determine if anything creates a barrier to use or if anything can assist in use. If you decide that you should have special equipment, make a list and shop it around to the town's local service organizations—you will be surprised at the financial help you may be able to get to put the equipment in to ensure that all people can effectively use your resources.

The building itself can be a barrier and you can work to change that. Having a ramp or ground-floor access to the building itself is the most obvious way to ensure that everyone can come in. If you don't have a handicapped entrance, make one a top priority. Be sure that there is adequate and handy parking for those with disabilities.

If you do have a ramp or ground-floor entrance, look at your door width and the manner in which your door (or doors, if you have a closed-in foyer) opens. Can the door handle be reached by someone in a wheelchair? If you have a closed-in foyer, does the second door open into the building? (A door opening into a closed-in foyer can present difficulties for the handicapped. Finally, be sure that you keep all paths and stairways free from obstacles such as snow, ice, bicycles, bookdrops, and so on.

The Interior

When your patrons come into your building, can they tell they're in a library? That might sound like an odd question but I have seen libraries that seem almost ashamed that they have bookshelves and computer stations. Some, although quite beautiful, look more like the Hanging Gardens of Babylon. Striking just the right balance between form and function can be more difficult than you think.

If some libraries err on the side of botany over books, others look dismally like the libraries of old, all dark wood and low lighting. The circulation desk still stands like a sentinel's post in front of the stacks, and new patrons aren't really sure if they must ask permission to trespass beyond to the books.

COME ON IN AND MAKE YOURSELF AT HOME!

Creating a welcoming environment affects the way your patrons use the library. If you'd like them to stick around for a while to study, browse, ask questions, or just enjoy themselves, you need to have an atmosphere conducive to long and pleasant visits. Light, airy and spacious rooms help to create that atmosphere, as will anticipating the needs that users of your facility might have.

In addition to making the library feel immediately comfortable even to those who are brand-new users, you have a great chance to market your materials by the layout and design of the interior space. Front-facing shelving, lots of eye-catching displays, comfortable seating, spotlighting, and bold signage will show your collection to its best advantage and make it feel more accessible to the public. As a community center, it's important that people coming into the library really do want to stay. They should be able to tell that the library has a wide variety and range of resources and that they can probably get what they need. It also helps if they feel that the library's organization is intuitive—that they don't need to get directions to find everything they're looking for.

There are easy and relatively inexpensive steps you can take to improve the atmosphere of your library. Cosmetic improvements are simple solutions to some problems that you may overlook as you become increasingly used to your library. Other solutions have a direct impact on how easy it is for people to use the library. These can range from the nearly impossible such as moving your shelving further apart to make wider aisles, to the easily achievable.

SIGNS

One simple way to make your library more user friendly is to install a signage system. Some people don't like to ask questions, and sometimes it's not even clear where one might ask questions anyway. Signs will ensure that patrons who come into your building *do* know where they are. In addition, directional signs will provide information on how to get to the place in the library they want to be. It's ironic that while we are in the information business, we are not always forthcoming with information on how to use our own facilities.

Sign systems can range from the very sophisticated (i.e., expensive) to the very simple (i.e., less expensive, but not cheap). If you decide you do need a sign system in your library, begin to investigate the options open to you. A signage or graphics company that specializes in libraries can probably help you determine your needs and will probably be able to set you up with a pretty spiffy set of signs. They will also make you gasp and choke when they give you a cost estimate.

You should also talk to the local trophy and sign shop to see what they can do. You will have to do all the work of deciding just what signs you need and where they should be placed, but you will be able to order professional-looking signs at a much lower (but not cheap) price.

Whatever you do, think twice about hand printing your signs. The whole idea of taking a good objective look at your library building is to find ways to improve it. Although *any* signs will be helpful, unless you have real talent available to you, homemade jobs are bound to look as cheap as they are and I'm not sure that in the end this will have been money well saved. If image wasn't important, the appearance of your facility wouldn't matter. We all know, however, that image *is* important. If we want to be treated as a professional institution, we should look like one.

COLOR AND LIGHT

It seems to me that nothing is more dramatic than the difference between a dark room and one that is filled with light. Dark often connotes elements of gloom, oppression, severity. Light, on the other hand, is often associated with an airy, open atmosphere. Given that libraries are places where people seek intellectual illumination, why not reflect that in our buildings?

Take a good look at your walls. Are they clean and bright? A new paint job in light colors can be quite inexpensive especially if you can hire your custodian to take on the job on an overtime basis. On the other hand, your Friends might take on the project themselves. You might even consider organizing the job, using volunteers from the community working during the course of several weekends. It probably goes without saying that if you don't have professional painters do the job, you will have to commit some of your own or staff members' time to be sure the enterprise is well organized and well structured. You want to be sure that it's done neatly and within a reasonable amount of time.

If, even with a new light paint job, your library is still dark, you might consider changing the lighting system (call in a lighting consultant for this), or the solution might be as simple as cutting down the foliage that has grown up outside the library's windows. Nothing is as pleasant as natural sunlight, and it makes sense to ensure that nothing obstructs its shining inside your library.

KEEPING IT CLEAN

Most of us understand how clutter can detract from any room's atmosphere. The first thing real estate agents will tell you to do to increase the appeal of your home to potential buyers is to paint the walls and get rid of the clutter. Apply that same reasoning to your library. Are your window sills piled high with magazines or pamphlets? Do you have more tables in a room than are ever filled by your patrons? Do you have displays and posters up that are turning yellow from time? Open your eyes and look around. Determine what can go and then show no mercy. Pamphlets and other ephemera should be weeded as diligently as your library's book collection—in fact, more diligently. Ephemera by their very nature are typically of very fleeting importance.

COMFORT

As important as pleasant and light surroundings are, comfort is equally so. I have found in my own library that the more nooks and crannies we have available for leisure reading or private study, the more people come and stay at the library. While you are somewhat locked in by the physical constraints and the necessary space taken up by your book collections, you might rearrange the furniture to provide a more private or cozy reading area or to accommodate group study.

When surveying your library for user comfort, don't leave out the children's room. Here some special needs exist. Children like to lounge around, and you can certainly accommodate that. Bright oversized throw pillows tossed in corners will get plenty of use. Think about providing a comfortable rocking chair for parents with infants, and don't forget a changing table (for obvious reasons you will want to make this available in a place convenient to, but at a distance from, the normal activity in the children's room).

No matter how terrific your service and collection are, if you do not have a library that is inviting and welcoming, your patrons are unlikely to stay. I think back on that librarian in the past who vociferously believed that patrons *shouldn't* stay (they just get in the way, you know), but we all know that when people stick around, they end up getting much more from their library. In-depth studying can be done with convenient access to all the materials that might help them. Reference service is right on hand to help patrons utilize the collection and to assist them with the computers. Browsing takes on a new dimension when it can be appreciated for its own intrinsic value. In addition to that, people who actually stay for a while will probably have stronger feelings of support for their library than people who don't.

ARTWORK AT THE LIBRARY

While you do want to get rid of stuff that's been sitting around forever and reshelve or relocate the materials that are valuable to the collection, it's reasonable and desirable to enhance the library's appearance through art and displays that are attractive and eye-catching. Displaying beautiful art may in itself be challenging. Where are you going to find the money? Ingenuity is the answer here.

Consider, for example, poster art. The graphics division of the American Library Association has produced some fine posters worthy of framing, and they have the added advantage of furthering the mission to promote library services. Ask the Friends group to consider footing the bill to frame some of your favorite posters. Talk to the people at your local frame shop to find out what you can do that will look nice and yet keep the cost low. Find out if they can set you up with frames that will allow for the changing of posters from time to time and do change those posters so the look is fresh.

Another way to provide your library with quality artwork at no cost is to seek out local artists and offer them the library as a place to show their work. Clearly outline what you are willing to accept and what the terms of art display will be. The quality of local artwork can vary considerably, but if your objective is to provide these artists with space as well as to enhance your library walls, then this might not matter. It's up to you and your trustees to determine what is acceptable. When you make that decision, you need to put it in writing in the form of policy. All artists need to be aware of the limits of the library's responsibility with regard to loss or destruction of their work. Similarly, you will be wise to specify a time limit so that a variety of artists will get a chance to show at the library.

DISPLAYS

Displays are another excellent way of adding interest to the library's interior and are wonderful promotions for your collection and services as well. The key to making displays attractive and effective is to be sure they are well done and rotated on a regular basis.

The ideas for creative displays are as limitless as the subject matter in your library. If you're new at the game, you can get some great ideas by looking in store windows. Not just bookstore windows (although they are often experts at highlighting their materials) but clothes shops, card shops, toy shops—any place that has a flair. Take a look at what other libraries are doing and borrow those ideas shamelessly. Finally, use your own imagination and that of your staff; tapping into your own creative talents is one of the intangible responsibilities of your job.

If you are displaying library materials, be sure that these materials can be taken from the display and checked out. You can make this possible by keeping a ready supply of related backup materials. Also, remember that your display will not be that impressive or eye-catching if it consists *only* of books. Bring in some objects that are related to the subject, to add interest. If you are not very artistic, find someone on staff or among your Friends or volunteers who is. A display that is unimaginative and uninspired does nothing to entice readership—and may well cement an image that libraries are not places of creativity and verve. One of the best library displays I have seen is one that highlighted a mystery collection. Inside clear plastic boxes (about three feet square) on which the books perched, were gloves, a magnifying glass, a "bloody" knife, and other objects of crimes committed and crimes solved.

If you have a display case, you might want to make it available for public use. This can really increase the creativity and diversity of your displays and save you some time. Letting others use this space is especially effective if you don't have a lot of artistic talent. A little digging could unearth a plethora of collectors in your town. Personal collections can range from baseball cards to old coins, political campaign paraphernalia, or great "finds" at yard sales. The main advantage of making your display case available to members of the community is that you can get a wide variety of interesting displays. The disadvantage is that you might open yourself up to providing space for the promotion of causes. As a public forum, you and your trustees might feel that this is just fine. You might decide, on the other hand, to limit the types of uses for the display case. Whatever you decide, the policy should be stated in writing in advance and should be applied equally to all. As with the artwork policy, you should detail your liability for loss or destruction, and you will want to limit the amount of time a single display can be shown.

Moving Walls, Raising Ceilings

While there is probably a lot you can do to enhance the atmosphere in your library cosmetically, there are other considerations for ease of use that will be beyond your control to change—at least in the near future. Even if you are stuck with a library that has a rabbit warren of corridors, a tower four stories high, or shelves bolted to the floor and ceiling and standing only two feet apart, you should not ignore the problems these physical constraints present.

You never know when you will have an opportunity to change a bad situation in your library's layout. If you are not even cognizant of the situation being bad in the first place, however, you are not as likely to recognize an opportunity when it does come along.

SPATIAL RELATIONSHIPS

Traffic patterns, while not easily manipulated, are an important consideration in helping patrons use your library easily. Obviously, you don't want people to have to wend their way through stacks of books before coming upon the circulation desk. Your public access computers should be located where they are handy both to the collection and to staff members who help patrons use the collection or online resources. New books should be convenient and visible.

Few functions in your library operate in isolation. Reference service might include heavy use of the nonfiction collection, for example, and the two collections should, therefore, be located within easy reach of one another. The young adult collection should not be housed on a floor different from the children's room if the person responsible for young adult services is the children's librarian. The circulation desk should be centrally located and easily accessible to all portions of the building.

Even if you are not satisfied with the current layout of the library, the thought of moving entire collections can be daunting, and anyone should think seriously before employing the energy that would be necessary to make major changes. Given the physical limitations of the building, in fact, it may be that imperfect spatial relationships are the best you can do. Again, consider signs, at least in the meantime, as a way of directing patrons through the various sections of your library, especially when collections and staff that logically should work together are separated geographically.

BARRIERS TO USE

Even if you have ensured that patrons can find various collections with the greatest ease possible, you could well have physical barriers within the library itself that you want to work to overcome. We are all aware that if the library is on more than one level, there should be access to all those levels for patrons who are unable to use the stairs. The simple yet costly solution is an elevator. If you do not already have one, you should make plans now to get one. The money might not be readily available, but it is a good idea to have plans for an elevator on file. A less costly method of transporting people from floor to floor is by chair lift. If it looks like an elevator is out of the question any time in the near future, you might look into the possibility of a chair lift. Check with other public buildings that have them to find out the pros and cons of such a scheme. You may find that they are far from ideal. They are inconvenient for strollers and overloaded parents, for example, and many people are very reluctant or embarrassed to use them.

While getting from floor to floor is an obvious problem, there are other barriers in all libraries that are less obvious. Technology has thrown open the doors to an infinite amount of information that is not site-dependent. We offer our patrons remote access to all that online technology can bring—well, at least those who can get to and use this technology. Assistive technology exists to help those who have disabilities use the library's resources. Large-screen computers, reader-computers, appropriately sized workstations are all available to help us make sure that everyone has access.

In addition to technology, what about our traditional collections? Do you have books on shelves just a couple of inches from the floor? Imagine putting on a pair of bifocals to read the spines, or how difficult it would be for someone on crutches or with a cane to stoop down to those volumes—and get back up again. While it makes sense for academic and special library collections to be shelved up 6½ feet high, it doesn't make sense for a public library. Whereas in an academic or research setting, most patrons look up just the title they need and then go get it, in a public library people browse. It's very hard to browse a 6½ foot shelf when you're five feet tall.

When it comes to furniture and assistive technology, it's imperative for us to find the resources to make them available. Though funding is always an issue, our society has placed a priority on the very issue that libraries are built upon—equal access—so there are likely to be grants or earmarked funding at the state and federal level for you to address barriers to use. Your town, too, is likely to support your efforts to ensure that all people regardless of physical ability, can access the materials and resources in their library—in fact, continuously working to ensure access for all is the law. Nevertheless, the reality is often that this money is not abundant, and the competition for it is often stiff. There is nothing more impressive than a plan that is well thought out and prepared in advance. You will have an advantage in showing that you have felt this need prior to the availability of money. This plan will also help lay the foundation for grants or appeals for gifts to help you provide the assistance "differently-abled" patrons need to use the library.

TYPES OF SPACES

In order to respond to the diversity of demand put upon the library, there should be a diversity of space. When you think of each use a patron makes of your facility, you will probably be surprised at the different kinds of spaces needed to best accommodate that use. Rows and rows of book shelves made sense 20 years ago, but books are now only a part of a library's overall services. People come in to study, to visit with friends, to go online, to enjoy a program, to read the daily news, as well as to check out materials. The space you provide should accommodate all these needs.

Quiet study areas can serve the special needs of your patrons as can areas for research and comfortable reading. The children's room should be located where it is incorporated into the general business of the library but where a greater degree of noise and activity is possible without disrupting other library users.

The provision of a meeting space has become a traditional component of library service. While the benefits of a meeting room for library programs are obvious, the way in which library meeting rooms serve the library's mission might be less so. When you think about the public library's goal to facilitate and encourage learning and intellectual exploration, you can see how clearly meeting space serves that mission. It is clear that not all information and ideas are transmitted via books, online technology, or other media; such transition also happens when people have the opportunity to get together to discuss a common topic.

You can offer your community an opportunity to share special knowledge or discuss beliefs in an open forum when you make a library meeting room available. Because this sharing is in accord with a public library's mission, I feel that it would be wrong to charge the public for its use. (See "Free Versus Fee" in Chapter 5, pages 130–132.) If the provision of meeting-room facilities *is* a component of general library service, then you would be creating barriers to some of your patrons if you charged a fee for their use.

Setting a policy for use of the meeting room is very important. Recently, *who* is entitled to use a library's meeting room has been a topic for hot debate. The question of separation of church and state comes into play if religious groups, for example, are allowed to meet. Life would be a lot simpler (and a lot less interesting) if two moral goods never came into conflict. Deciding to allow religious groups to use the library's space is a perfect example of this conflict. It gets even trickier when a group's agenda is hateful or politically unpopular. Sticking to a policy of neutrality can be difficult, but it is important.

I feel very strongly that *all* groups should be allowed equal access to meeting rooms regardless of their agenda, beliefs or cause. The library collection itself is a reflection of a wide array of beliefs. We make space available on our shelves for fundamentalism and atheism alike; we seek out and welcome materials that support all points of view; we go out of our way to accommodate the entire spectrum. We do this because most of us believe that banning potentially offensive ideas is more harmful than allowing their expression. We cannot be a thoughtful and self-determining society unless we have access to, and give voice to, the broadest possible range of ideas. We do not consider this a "church and state" issue or a "right from wrong" issue. We consider it an issue of access and intellectual freedom. Whether an idea is presented in a book or in a lecture or discussion, these issues remain the same. Regardless of the means of delivery, if we intend to uphold the principles of intellectual freedom we should not deny the message.

The trick in safeguarding the rights of all those who use the meeting room is to set up a policy whereby one set of rules is equally applied to all groups. You can avoid becoming a house of worship by limiting the number of times any group can use the room. You can eliminate commercial enterprises by insisting that *all* meetings held at the library must be free and open to the public. With those two fundamental rules in place, you need only specify rules for cleaning and security. (See Appendix L—Sample Meeting Room Policy.)

While you are considering patrons' space needs, don't forget our own. Being the public-spirited, self-sacrificing types that we librarians often are, it is typical to find that while great effort is put forth to accommodate comfortable and easy use of a library by its patrons, the work room is a veritable disaster area. Cartons of books line the walls; computers, old broken-down office equipment, printers, and miscellaneous papers cover every conceivable space. Does this scenario sound familiar to you? If so, you can feel some comfort in knowing you are not alone—then you can roll up your sleeves and make some changes.

Ideally, every library should have plenty of work space behind the scenes. There should be countertops along the walls and work tables clear of debris, with shelves for incoming materials, cataloged materials and materials ready to go out to the public. In the ideal world, there should be comfortable and separate work stations for the members of your staff, with up-to-date computers and equipment in good working order. Each member of the staff should have at least a nook to call his own and a place to take a quiet and relaxing break away from the business of the library.

In reality, many small libraries were not designed with the library staff in mind. In some very small libraries, there is a sense of achievement in having turned a janitor's closet into a staff washroom. In very, very small libraries, the work room and janitor's closet may be combined! The idea of adequate, clutter-free space for all the "behind the scenes" functions and the people who perform them is only a dream. The fact of the matter is, work space of any kind in small public libraries is usually at a premium.

Given this reality, it makes sense to work within the limitations you may have, to create the best situation out of a poor one—and prospects don't have to be dismal. If you have a crowded, cluttered work room, gear up for a massive and merciless clean-up effort. Get the entire staff involved, and put the person who never saves a thing in charge. (Just be sure your resident pack rat is there, too, to ensure that primary source records kept from your town's original settlement aren't thrown out with the old order lists.) Get rid of everything you haven't used for years and don't have an immediate or specific future need for. Don't bother saving anything that may come in handy for something someday. *Today* you need room, you need organization.

Once you have done a thorough cleaning, organize the remaining space as best you can. Think about the work flow. Where do books get delivered and opened? How is the shipment checked against the order files, and who does that? Where are books cataloged, and where are they covered? Arrange the space you have to accommodate this routine efficiently. Consolidate, condense, and label everything. The work will flow more smoothly for everyone if the work room is organized.

Issue an edict that from now on everyone must clean up after himself immediately. A pair of scissors left out today will lead to a few pages of construction paper left on the table until "later" tomorrow. Eventually, you will have a mess again, and a feeling of being overwhelmed by your lack of space.

Look around to see how you can arrange work area desks and tables in a way that gives the workers a sense of space. For a relatively small investment you can buy small desks and computer stands so that work "stations" are created. Studies in ergonomics show that productivity and job satisfaction are increased when working conditions are optimized. Don't think of your staff's comfort and ease in performing their jobs as a subordinate concern to serving the public. Once you give your staff the consideration they are due with regard to their work areas, you may elect to annex a part of the public space for staff. A radical, but perhaps ultimately wise, decision.

Time to Build

The time may come when you recognize that computers seem to be taking over every spare inch of space you have, when you are thinking about designing 10' towers for your AV collection, when you are shifting the books on the shelves with a greater frequency than usual, when you become a little more relentless in weeding, and you notice that most of your tables have been replaced with additional shelving. It can be a sinking feeling when you come face to face with the fact that your library has become too small. It's likely that you've seen it coming for some time now, but admitting it means you'll have to do something about it. Something major.

When you first realize without any doubt that you will have to either add on or build a new library in order to maintain your current level of service—and certainly to increase it—you have two options. The first—and this *will* occur to you— is to find another job! The more you know about library construction, the more appealing this option is likely to be.

When this notion subsides, however, you'll take a closer look at the second option—to square your shoulders and face the real possibility of a construction project. As tempting as ignoring or running away from the problem might seem at first, there is probably no other single occasion in your professional life that will offer you the opportunity to effect such tangible and long-term change for your community. Here is your ticket to immortality, so grab it and do yourself proud.

HOW CAN YOU TELL?

How will you know for sure when additional space is needed? The signs will be obvious to you and your staff long before they are to the public. Unfortunately, while it would be ideal to begin expansion when the signs first appear, the reality is that you probably won't be able to sell the public on the idea until they have to leapfrog over makeshift shelving, trip over make-do computer wiring, and vault the additional magazine rack in the lobby in order to get to the circulation desk.

You, however, will tune into the more subtle initial signs. At first there will be the necessity removing yet another table to install a new computer station or two.

You will begin shelving books on shelves just inches from the floor. As time goes by, you will find that the amount of "free" space at the end of each shelf gradually decreases to almost none. When there is no more space to sit and read, when books are crammed into every available inch of shelf space, when every conceivable space in your library has been given up to computer stations or makeshift shelving, you will know.

It is very important to start making the case for more space as soon as you begin to anticipate the need, even if it isn't readily apparent to others. In town reports, to civic groups, in newspaper columns and casually to your patrons, let the word out. Your town is unlikely to act right away, but when the need becomes too pressing to ignore any longer, your past predictions will lend credibility to your claim that planning for additional space must begin *now*.

THE WORK BEGINS

As the need for more space becomes apparent to you, you should discuss the matter with your trustees. Have a preliminary report available showing them the trends in library usage over the years, the growth of your community, and the minimum standards for shelving, seating and work room space, and show them by what extent you fall short in meeting the standards.

Convincing the trustees that your need for additional space is valid will be the first of many steps to take in achieving your goal of a larger library. Once you have convinced them you should *get a library building consultant*. This is no time to wing it. A good consultant will show you how to identify and articulate your needs, how to make the case to the community, what avenues for funding exist, and how to get the job done. Contact other libraries in your state that have recently built and talk to the people at the state library. In some states, building consultants are available through the state library; in others, the state library will make recommendations for private consultants.

In addition to a building consultant, you should work with the trustees to organize a building committee, consisting of the building consultant, at least one of your trustees, several high-profile, well respected people in the community, a lawyer and someone involved in the construction business. Most important, you should be sure that *you* are included in the building committee as the chair. There is no one else who knows your needs better than you, and a successful building will depend on you and your staff's diligent input.

It is wise to keep the building committee fairly small. You don't want a bureaucracy here, you want a working committee that gets things done. Each person you ask should be aware that this will be a time-consuming as well as important and prestigious committee. Be sure that every member is committed. It is also wise to ask one member to serve as recording secretary or to tape record each session. This can be important later if there are disputes about what was agreed to. Not all changes and modifications will be put in writing no matter how committed you are to doing that from the outset. Having good records of all meetings will serve as memory for the project itself, as well as for posterity.

THE FIRST DECISION

After the committee's initial interview with your building consultant, you will have a better idea of what options to explore. The first decision to be made is whether you want to add on to the existing building or whether it makes more sense to build on a new site altogether. Building an addition is often the better (easier) choice. Your library is probably centrally located. In addition, it is likely that the people in your community have a strong attachment to the building itself. Finally, with an addition, you eliminate the need to search for and purchase a building lot. Even if you must buy adjacent land to add on (assuming such land exists), the search itself is eliminated as is the PR job that will be necessary if you are moving the library to an entirely new location.

It is possible that the library's existing site will not accommodate a new addition. The need to search for a new location is unalterable if there is absolutely no available land for building. You will have a more difficult time if there is *some* additional space, but it is so confining that it will severely limit the type and size of your addition. In this case, it makes sense to fight as hard as you can for a new location. Increasing the size of your library, whether by addition or new construction, is going to mean an incredible amount of time, effort and money for a lot of people. It is foolish to go to all the trouble just to end up with an addition that does not meet your needs or one that will only solve your space problems for a few more years.

If you need to find a new location for your library and you are successful in making that case, be sure to work with your building consultant to identify the characteristics a good site must provide. Such things as visibility, ample parking, and central location all need to be considered. It is also a good idea to bring someone in from your town's planning department, who will know what land is available and what land has good development potential. It will save a lot of time and a lot of bad feelings if town officials participate in the location of your new library.

THE BUILDING PROGRAM

Once you have the trustees on your side, a building consultant on retainer (the Friends of the Library might help with fees if necessary), and a building committee committed to the project, you need to write a building program. If you are good at writing you can do this yourself. Committee writing can take forever, but you will want a lot of input from all staff members and from patrons who have good insight into issues of traffic flow, intuitive use, and need for flexibility and use of technology.

Of course writing a building program is standard work for a building consultant, but with your consultant's guidance and provision of a template, you can save good money if you put it together yourself.

The building program is a document that will clearly state what additional space you need and why you need it. It will give an estimate of how much additional space will accommodate anticipated needs for the next twenty years. The building program will outline how the library functions and what spaces need to work in concert.

A well-written building program will serve you in several ways. Primarily, this document is meant to direct an architect's plan, because it will show what you need for every aspect of library operation and service. In fact, however, the building program can work extremely well as a promotional and campaign tool as well. In all probability, you will have to convince a lot of people that your need is not only legitimate but desperate! A well-written program will convey this message with facts and figures and not just a "because I say so."

A good building program can also be an invaluable fundraising device. If you are planning to financially support the new construction (wholly or in part) through fundraising, you will need to have information showing why new construction is necessary and what current problems this new construction will solve. All this information will be provided in your building program.

The first one or two pages of your building program should begin with your mission statement and continue as an essay broadly describing your library—its history, its present condition and what you imagine will be needed for the future. Include a statement or two about your library's beginnings—when it was founded and how many people it served. If your library saw expansion of any kind over the years, describe it and tell how it served the library.

Move from that history into a description of your present state. How many people are currently served by your library? How many adults, how many children? Explain in what ways you find yourselves in need of additional space. Be specific. Explain what your crowded conditions mean for your workers and your patrons. You should state, for example, that the work room originally designed for one must now accommodate four employees. Explain that emerging and growing information technology comes with unique and significant space and wiring needs. Talk about how popular books are stored in the attic, study space for patrons has been taken over by shelves, books are stored on windowsills and on the floor.

Finally, as part of the introductory essay to your building program, explain what you hope to accomplish by building. Give the current square footage of your library and estimate what additional space will be needed to enable you to carry your tradition of service into the next two decades. Tell your readers what circulation was when the library was first built, what it was twenty years ago and what it is currently. Include figures from census records on how your community has grown over the years, and compare those figures to your own rise in patronage. In short, use this introduction to give the facts about your library's service and to persuade anyone who reads it that the request for more space is legitimate.

Following the one to two page introduction to your building program, you may want to include a page or two of charts. If you have experienced dramatic growth over the years, that growth will be visible and impressive if shown by graph. Include growth of circulation, visits to the library, population, use of online resources, patronage and perhaps even hours open—whatever you feel will clearly show your library's success over the years that has brought you to this point.

Your next objective will be to describe each individual space in your library: how it is used, who uses it, and to what degree it may be insufficient for its purpose. For example, your description of the reference area might look something like this:

> Technology has made dramatic changes in the way the library delivers information and reference services. While print resources are still a critical component of this service, online resources are growing in their importance and their use both by staff and by the public.
>
> The reference collection and public computer lab is housed in the northeast corner of the lobby. Currently there are 105 linear feet of shelf space available to house a collection of approximately 700 volumes. Library standards suggest 156 linear feet for a collection of this size. Due to a lack of adequate shelf space, it has become necessary to withdraw one volume for each new volume added.
>
> Recently, additional space has been given over to a public access computer lab consisting of five individual work stations. This new service was accommodated by the removal of two tables and eight chairs for study and research. Further, because this area is shared with the new books collection, the periodical collection and current newspaper collection, high patron traffic often makes quiet research and study impossible.

Other areas to be discussed are the stack areas for fiction and nonfiction, the children's collection, the young adult collection, audiovisual materials, office areas, work room(s), circulation desk, staff lounge, meeting room, and special collections (such as state or genealogical collections). In addition to a brief description of these spaces and their inadequacies, you should provide a statement of security and other general architectural considerations. This would include the need for emergency exits, the ability to monitor the patrons who enter and leave the library, access for the handicapped into the building and throughout the interior, the need for book-drops, coat racks, janitor's room and storage, clocks, alarms, etc. Be sure to stipulate that adequate wiring and electrical flexibility are critically important as your technological infrastructure will surely grow and change in coming years.

You will also want to convey the importance of preserving the good parts of the existing library. You may have such things as stained glass windows, wainscoting, or a beautiful old oak circulation desk that you want to preserve or save for the new building. Be sure to address these considerations in the building program.

When writing the document, keep in mind that you want more than just additional space. You want space that works well for you. Many architects have little (if any) experience with libraries. It's up to you to be clear about how a library functions and what spaces must work together for ease of operation. You and I know that the room for children's programs should not be located two flights up from the children's room, but the architect might not. It's important for you to include a flow chart in your program that explains different aspects of your service. For example, a flow chart showing how books make it onto the shelves is helpful. Begin with the reading of reviews (and where that's done) and proceed through the ordering of the books, where they are delivered, who checks them in, where they are catalogued, and where they are covered and delivered for patron access. All these tasks raise important issues for planning work space.

A chart showing what spaces should be adjacent or could be separated from others should be included. You don't want to have to send an architect back to the drawing board because he put the circulation desk on the second floor with new books in the basement. Be clear in showing how and why spatial relationships are important. Don't assume the architect knows anything about how you'd like your library to function.

Finally, you need to provide a "facility checklist" for each space you have addressed in your building program (see Appendix M—Facility Checklist). The facility checklist represents the nuts and bolts of what you need. Based on both standards for space (see bibliography) and your predictions for use over the next twenty years, this sheet will spell out just how much space you need for each area. It will show how many people typically use the area, how many volumes will be shelved, how the space use is broken down, and what the spatial relationship to other areas must be, as well as requirements for lighting, sound, utilities (phone, computer terminals, etc.), and requirements for temperature control. You should also outline what kind of furniture will be needed in this space, both fixed and moveable.

It will be valuable if at the end of your building program you include a very brief bibliography of works you used in determining standards for space and shelving requirements, as well as information you used to determine future growth for your community (such as census reports and predictions). This will help the architect if he is trying to verify or wishes to modify a space requirement, and it will lend credibility to your report.

Funding or Architect— Which Comes First?

When you finish the building program you will probably feel like you have already done more work than any one person should have to do. The truth is, you have just begun. Now that you have clearly articulated your needs, you will have to have someone translate those needs into a workable plan, and you will need funding to turn the plans into a new and wonderful library—details, details!

Whether the architectural plans or the funding for the project comes first seems to vary with each library. If you have the money to hire an architect to draw conceptual plans based on the needs set forth by the building program, you will have something concrete to show the public. In addition to that (if the plans are basically acceptable to the building committee), you will then have a good idea how much money will be needed for the project.

A note here: *Always, always overestimate how much you think the building will cost.* You remember Murphy and his laws? Well he's really in his element here. It's a well known principle that building always takes longer and costs more than even the most conservative estimates predicted. It might be tempting to go with the lower estimate because you think that it will be an easier sell to the community. In reality, however, it is probably as hard to get $5,000,000 as it is to get $5,300,000. In fact, if you believe the project will cost $5,000,000, you might try going for $5,500,000 and compromise at $5,300,000. That way you have a chance of staying under budget and being regarded as a real hero.

If you have no money to hire an architect for conceptual drawings, and you feel that you cannot possibly raise the money prior to a bond issue, you will have to estimate the cost based solely on square footage requirements. While the publication *Means Square Foot Costs* (the annual guide to construction costs for different regions in the United States) will give the average square foot cost of construction in your area, it should be taken as a very broad estimate only. Use it in conjunction with the price tag for similar sized additions or new construction of libraries in your area—and again, overestimate.

If you get the funding prior to the plans, this funding will influence the type of building the architect designs. In fact, this can force some ingenious thinking and more careful planning on the part of the architect and the building committee. I've even heard there's such a thing as having too much money when building, though I don't happen to know of a library that can boast of it. It's comforting to think that limited funds might be a good thing.

Finding Funds

Funding for a new library or a library addition can come from gifts and grants, or it can be tax money resulting from a bond issue or referendum. Most likely it will be a combination of the above. In a small town, it is pretty unlikely that you will be able to raise *all* the money necessary for additional library space (at least in your own lifetime) unless a person of stupendous means dies and leaves his fortune to your library. In the real world, the money you need for library construction will probably be a combination of fundraising and public taxes.

FUNDRAISING

If you plan to finance the construction to any great degree through fundraising, hire a professional fundraiser. The building committee and the trustees might be tempted to try to save money by foregoing professional help. Even though many of these committee members will recommend bypassing a professional fundraiser, none—I repeat *none*—is likely to take on the project himself.

It's no surprise that no one is likely to volunteer to take this on. It's a whole lot of work. People are busy; they may be willing to *help*, but they don't want to be the chief of this particular tribe—and let me tell you, neither do you! You have a library to run, remember? You've got books to order, morale to boost, feathers to smooth, and questions to answer. Professional fundraisers make the money they do because a major campaign can be a full-time project. If you and your trustees are bent on getting a good amount of the money through fundraising, get qualified help.

Even if you do convince the powers-that-be to hire a professional fundraiser, make it clear that there will still be a lot of work for the committee and volunteers to do. Alas, fundraisers don't actually go out and get the money for you; they teach you and your volunteers how to do it. They organize the campaign, they help you put together a case statement, and they help you identify the potential major donors. The legwork must still be done by you and yours.

In the end, if fundraising is going to be your sole method, be absolutely sure you have a volunteer who is willing to work with a fundraiser in organizing and managing the campaign. Capital fundraising is *not* in your job description (or shouldn't be), so don't get roped in. Also realize that if you don't have someone who is extremely committed to putting in time and a half for the next six months to a year, the whole thing could fall through and you'll be back at square one.

GOING FOR TAX SUPPORT

If you plan to finance new library construction through a bond issue or referendum, you, your trustees and your building committee still have a lot of work to do. While you won't be going out into the community asking for money directly, you will still be asking the community for money. Timing is important, as is a good, honest and well-articulated campaign.

If you believe you may have a difficult time getting a positive vote for funding, you may want to consider engaging a local public relations firm to help you design a campaign. Though this will likely be costly, the Friends or a library benefactor may see it as worth funding. If the amount you spend on professional assistance translates into a "yes" vote for the library, the investment will have been well worth it. A professional firm can help you map out a strategy, come up with a catchy slogan, and do some "market research" to determine (1) if the voters are supporters, and (2) what message would persuade them to vote "yes." They can also develop some glossy brochures and even some public service announcements for radio and television. A note of caution here, however: If you decide to wage a more glitzy and professional campaign, be sure to indicate on all the public materials that they were funded by the Friends of the Library or by private contributions. You don't want the public to think you are so well funded already that you don't need further taxpayer support.

When you begin to make plans for a bond issue or referendum, contact your mayor or town manager to find out what is required. Ask to be put on the town council or select board's agenda to discuss the matter. This will be your first campaign speech. Don't go it alone. Ask a board member and the most influential member of the building committee to accompany you.

In your presentation, make it clear how serious the lack of space has become (of course, having done your groundwork, you've been warning them about this for several years now). Tell them how much your library is used and how its services have grown. If you can persuade this group to be on your side, the battle will be half won. Even if you can't win them over, however, they won't be able to accuse you later of going behind their backs.

Once the town's officials know of your intentions, it's time to take your case to the public. Talk to every group in town who will listen. If you have conceptual drawings and models, show them off. Brag about your services. Make it clear that your need for more space is a direct result of your success in serving the public. Most important, let every group and person you talk to know what's in it for them.

When talking to the PTA, pitch the new children's room and how important computers and access to information technology is to every child's future. Talk about the amount of space the children need and the type of environment that will be conducive to their learning. Talk about the importance of reading for children and how that is part of your library's mission. Talk about the important role you play in supporting homework success. Explain what a new and larger children's room will mean for kids.

When you talk to the business community, let them know that a new reference room will enable you to expand your collection. Tell them it will accommodate database searching and access to a wide array of online resources. Talk to them about the possibility of small project study rooms equipped with computers and projectors and maybe even fax machines and copiers! Talk about the great business resources available to them, and the phone service for quick answers.

Talk to the garden club and tell them how you have had to store some wonderful books on gardening in the attic. Explain how you'd like to expand that collection because it's so popular, but you can't because of a lack of shelf space. Let them know a new library means new and better meeting room space for them as well as all organizations in the community.

Set a time line for your campaign and work hard to win. Use every method open to you to discuss your need and persuade the community that it is legitimate and worth paying for. Line up time on the local radio talk show. Be sure you have at least one article a month in your in-house newsletter describing how you've grown, what the consequences of overcrowding have been, and in what ways new space will solve the problems.

This campaign is not one you should wage alone. The more people you get on the bandwagon, the more successful the vote will be. The very first group to win to your side is the Friends group. They all have contacts in the community and will work to get public opinion on your side. Likewise, ask your volunteers to become familiar with your plans for expansion and to pass the word around town. Write articles in the newspapers that talk about the history and growth of the library. As you get closer to voting time, lay it on thick. You want your campaign to be strong but not too strong and so far in advance that opposition has time to coalesce.

If you work throughout the year to make your needs and plans known, you will have done all you can to win the vote for the library. As a last-minute effort, get Friends and volunteers to participate in a phone-tree and be sure that every registered patron of your library gets a call asking them to support new library construction.

Selecting the Architect and the Contractor

THE ARCHITECT

Whether you choose the architect prior to funding or not, the method is still basically the same. Your building consultant will explain how and where ads for architects should be made. If you're an official town department, there will be rules and procedures to guide you in issuing a request for a proposal (RFP). The design of a central civic building will be appealing to a lot of architects and you'll probably be inundated with queries to your initial advertisement.

Because it is likely that you will want to weed out some of the interested architects from the beginning, you will want to specify in the RFP that they list recent pertinent past jobs in their response as well as contact people from those jobs. You will see quickly who has, for example, no experience in designing public buildings. Call references they list and people who occupy the buildings they have designed. You will be surprised at what you hear—including horror stories of buildings that don't work and monumental architectural egos. The more hopefuls you can eliminate from the outset (assuming you get a good amount of response), the easier your final selection will be.

Once you have weeded out architects who don't satisfy your first set of criteria, send remaining candidates a copy of the building program. Ask them to set up an appointment with you to discuss in greater detail what you hope to accomplish with a new library or new library addition. See if it is possible for them to arrange for you and the building committee to go and visit some of their recent building projects. Set a deadline that is reasonable for them and for you; it will be interesting to see which architects work well within that deadline. After you have met with each prospective architect individually, you should set one or two days aside where you and the building committee interview each architect on a more formal basis.

You should ask that each one bring in conceptual ideas and an estimate of what his design and construction will cost (obviously, this will be an estimate, but be sure you know what he has based it on). The plans you select may end up changing a good deal before construction begins, but you will have an opportunity to see who best understands the needs expressed in the building program and has found creative and responsible ways to meet those needs. You can also get an idea how easy each architect will be to work with. If he is defensive about your questions, you would be wise to forget him.

A good working relationship will turn out to be crucial in getting a building you're really happy with, as I found out. However congenial and flexible the architect may be, you need to feel that you can be firm in your own demands. The plans for our addition went along quite well, with one exception. Our architect felt strongly that each room should be well defined—by walls. The stack areas in the plans were, therefore, enclosed with only a door leading into them. I expressed my strong opposition, citing the fact that we were not ashamed to have books—we wanted to show them off. I talked philosophically about access and invitation and how walls might indicate closed shelving.

Each revision of the plans found the walls up; at each subsequent meeting, I insisted they be removed. In the final drawings the walls were, finally, down. But you can bet when those stack areas were being built, I was right there on site, suspiciously eyeing any wallboard brought to the area! Happily, this was the only point where there was major dispute, but I was glad I was able to be firm and that in the end, the architect respected the wishes of those who actually have to live with the results.

The wide variety of designs, coupled with the different notions about what is best held by members of the building committee, can make final selection a tense time. Hopefully, you have stated your needs so clearly to this committee that they will opt for a functional building over one that will primarily be a community showplace (and little else).

Once you've selected the architect, it is time to start talking to construction companies? Not quite. Unless you've been able to hire the architect *before* the project was funded, you probably are still dealing with conceptual drawings and ideas. When it gets down to the real brass tacks of locating electrical outlets, installing water fountains and placing doors in work areas, you and your staff need to be there. Everyone who works at your library should be required to give input.

How would their jobs be made easier by new space? What problems do they experience in their current quarters? In what ways have they noticed patrons struggling to use the current facilities? The more input you and your staff have into the final design, the more likely you will not be saying "if only..." one year after the building is complete.

You will be working under time pressure, but be sure that the final architectural drawings reflect the needs of your staff and your library users. The time you spend now will pay you back a thousandfold in the coming years, and your successor will not cuss your name for having created (or failed to eliminate) a problem of function.

THE CONTRACTOR

When the plans have been finalized to everyone's satisfaction and the money is "in the bank," it is time to put the project out to bid. If you are using any tax money to support construction, it is probable that the town will be involved with this process. The town manager or director of public works will want to oversee the bid procedure and the town itself will probably be the entity to award the contract.

Putting a public building project out to bid is a fairly standard procedure and if a town official is not involved, the architect or building consultant can help your building committee with this phase of the project. The architect will have to ensure that a full set of plans is available to each interested contractor. A reasonable time limit will be set, as well as a specific time and date for opening the bids.

The opening of bids is, surprisingly, one of the most exciting (and tense) aspects of the entire project. You will be hoping that the bids, or at least one of them, will come in within budget. It's possible that the new building or addition has been designed with alternatives, in case cost-saving modifications have to be made. At this point, however, you are still hoping for the slate roof and marble trim. Within about 15 minutes, you will know whether you can break ground for the building of your dreams (and plans) or whether you will have to go back to the drawing board—possibly with the low bidder—to find out how you can get the costs in line. Welcome to the world of compromise!

Construction

Because the building committee has worked so carefully on the building program, because you selected an architect with good experience and excellent references, because you spent all the hours needed to go over the plans with a fine-tooth comb, incorporating good ideas from your staff and trimming where it made sense to, you have been able to come to terms with the contractor and are now ready to break ground.

It would be nice to say that all you need to do now is have the traditional groundbreaking ceremony and plug your ears, but the fact of the matter is that the construction itself will be a continually changing process that still requires a watchful eye. Just as a building consultant will facilitate the planning process and help you avoid disastrous mistakes, a clerk of the works will oversee the actual building process and ensure that the contractor is following the specifications carefully. This clerk works for you, and unless you or your staff members were construction workers in a past life, you need to have someone who ensures that cost-cutting changes are not being made as construction progresses. Unless the contractor you pick has done a lot of work for the town before with no complaints, it is wise to spend a little more money for this long-term insurance of quality construction.

Even with a clerk of the works on board, you shouldn't extricate yourself from the project at this point. Typically there will be periodic job meetings between the job supervisor, the clerk of the works, an architect's representative and you. This is primarily a time for giving progress reports, adjusting time lines and reporting problems or changes that need to be made. You need to be there when the job supervisor and the architect's representative blithely decide that you really don't need two doors in the children's room (even though one door leads to the program room and the other to the hallway). Every change that is made has the potential to affect the function of the building. Even though you have spent a lot of time with the architect on the project, expediency may make their memory short, and you may find that items in the plans that you stated were crucial come up for question and change.

Documenting for Posterity

Once the construction bid has been awarded, you should make sure that you document the work on the new library as it's being completed. If you are building a new addition, make a video tour of the existing building being sure to highlight all areas that will be expanded, renovated, or changed. If you are building a new facility, videotape the site prior to construction. Then, once a week or so, videotape the construction process. Be sure to get the interesting moments like the excavation of the site, the pouring of the foundation, the framing of the new structure, the carpeting, and the installation of shelves.

Not only will creating a tape be a wonderful gift to the future, it will be fun to show new patrons on opening day and you might even get a local public-interest television station to air it—or even some of it. In addition to the video record, be sure to take lots of snapshots as well so that you can create a scrapbook to be shared on opening day and into the future.

Celebrating

You may not believe this halfway through the project, but the day *will* come when construction is complete. The sense of pride and fulfillment you experience will make every agonizing hour spent over the past several years fade into forgiving memory. While the building is still new, you will be the recipient of kudos and praise. Go ahead, bask in it! Although this will feel a bit like a private victory (in your heart of hearts), you will know that in fact it is a public success.

You have lots of credit to hand around and you should be sure to do so. One of the most wonderful nights of my life was when we had a private reception for everyone directly involved with my building project. The architect and his representatives, the contractor and principals working on the project, the trustees, the staff, the executive board of the Friends and the town officials were all invited to come to the library the night before the official grand opening. We were able to convince two local restaurateurs to cater the evening, and the local chamber orchestra played softly in the background. Treat yourself and those involved to a special event like this; it may well be the last time for all of you to spend time together for quiet reflection and the expression of mutual pride.

The grand opening is the last item on your building agenda. It's a time for speeches and a time to show the library off in the best light possible. A grand opening will bring people who curiously eyed the construction during the past year into the library for the first time in their lives. Be sure you have plenty of help on hand to give out lots of new library cards.

The thing most people who come to the grand opening will want is to have a look around. Enlist members of your staff and volunteer crew to give guided tours that mention not only the befores and afters but how this *new* library will be able to meet their library needs much more efficiently. Once the tours are over (or before they even begin) take time to talk about the importance of libraries in general and yours in particular. See if you can get the governor or some other well-known, well-respected person to give a keynote address. Keep the number of speeches low and the speeches themselves short, but be sure you convey the message that this library belongs to the people of the community. The pride should be theirs.

FIVE

Service

What makes the public library viable in this new technological age? Why do we need libraries if everyone will eventually have Internet access? What makes libraries so special? It's service. Everything we do in managing public libraries conspires in the end to enable us to offer a service. We fight for better budgets, create Friends groups, promote the library, develop collections and maintain facilities, all in order to provide members of our community with good library service. It is not enough to offer a warehouse full of books. It's not enough to link a computer to the Internet. Despite the emerging technology—perhaps even because of it—our libraries are being used now more than ever because library staff and the services they provide add value to the learning experience.

We know that the Internet is just one avenue for finding information—a tremendous avenue. Librarians are more important than ever before, however, in helping patrons navigate through an enormous and growing collection of information sites. Librarians have a wealth of experience in evaluating information and selecting out of a universe of possibilities that which best meets individual needs. This experience and expertise is well valued by those who utilize our services. Furthermore, this expertise is becoming more greatly respected by those who have found that while the Internet does have tremendous capacity to inform, librarians can help sort through the information, evaluate it, put it into context, and provide supporting materials such as books.

In addition to serving the reference and research needs of our patrons, we are still the best source in town for leisure reading, children's programs, meeting space, study space, and browsing books both old and new. Our collections are not driven solely by the current market as bookstores are, we also provide books and materials that have retained their value over the years—books that would never retain their shelf space in an environment where profit is the number-one goal. A bumper sticker once offered through the Vermont Library Association said, "Libraries: Keepers of Tradition, Catalysts for Change." That says a lot about our services past and future. Because our role for service is so important in our communities, it is critical that it is the best it can possibly be.

It is likely that your library is already offering exemplary library service and your goals for service have been well articulated and are shared by everyone who works for the library. No matter how good your library service is, however, the world (and your part of it) is always changing, as are opportunities to serve. It is important, therefore, to consider planning, goal-setting, and assessment of service as ongoing projects. Every few years you should ask whether your library is taking advantage of all opportunities to serve the community and if some of your services need to be modified or discontinued in order to accommodate the new.

Why Are We Here Anyway?

In light of the changing world of information delivery, it seems reasonable to ask what kind of services public libraries should offer. How do we continue to stay relevant and viable in this changing landscape? There may be no other public agencies as creative as libraries in answering that question. As a matter of fact, I am not convinced that this creativity is always in the best interest of the library itself. For example, I know of libraries that have made valiant attempts to extend their service by offering for loan such things as lawn mowers and garden tools. I have no doubt that these kinds of offerings have been popular but then so, too, would be an ice-cream stand in August.

At the very least, this kind of activity should make us consider what it is libraries *should* be offering the public and where we draw the line on the services we choose to provide. Whether or not the tool trade is popular (or even profitable if tools are rented as a fundraising activity), it makes sense to consider the time and money such enterprises consume and, more importantly, the kind of image we will acquire as a result.

Libraries, as we who work for them will attest, are important and integral parts of the public education landscape. Public libraries provide a unique opportunity for members of the community to continue their intellectual growth without regard to qualifications, income, or philosophical predilections. What an amazing service! And much more impressive, I think, than dealing in hardware.

It is true that because not everyone uses their public library, we are underused. We know that many nonusers would benefit by library service if only we could get them in the door. The desire to do so makes a good case for considering new (or modifying old) services—but these services should be based on our mission to provide information, intellectual stimulation, independent learning opportunities and leisure reading to the public. Not only do we not need garden tools to enhance our mission, our mission could well be trivialized as a result of offering them.

Planning

Before any logical decision can be made as to what service to offer, it makes sense to do a little brainstorming with your staff, trustees and members of the community to see if common goals rise to the surface. You should try to reach agreement on what is within the scope of a public library's mission. How do you determine what *is* within the library's scope? How do you prioritize those services once they are identified? These are not questions to answer quickly or by yourself. Before deciding what to change, upgrade or implement, you should clearly state what you currently offer and how well it's being received. The categories to look at are user groups, collection strengths and weaknesses, hours open, staff structure and schedule, programs, outreach, and budget. Within each of these categories you should determine if you are doing all you can to deliver excellent library service.

User Groups

To begin with, look at your users, both present and potential. Determine who would benefit by library service in your community and who actually uses the library at present. Compare your patron-base profile to that of the town in general. Are their specific groups of people who are absent from your patrons? A growing minority population? Teens? New immigrants? Laborers? The elderly? Over time, your library may have found such a comfortable niche with a particular profile (e.g., white, middle-class, female) that you haven't given a lot of thought to new or different profiles in your community. Just as the world of information retrieval is changing dramatically, so is the demographic make-up of America—it could be happening right under your own nose and yet the library hasn't changed its service focus or offerings in years.

You may also find that you have a population especially at risk of failure because they are not literate or are barely so. One of the most important ways public libraries can combat illiteracy is to promote reading for babies. New parents and infants may be a potential user group that, to date, has not been targeted for special services by your library. Your community may have an active adult basic education initiative and your library may well be able to support their efforts by offering a special collection of high-interest, low-reading-level materials along with space for tutoring. Teens, too, can be a good target for illiteracy prevention efforts on the part of your library. If the drop-out rate in your community is high (and many would say one is too many), you might want to beef up services to teens and preteens especially targeting those who are not doing well in school. Mentoring programs, Teen Advisory Boards, social programs, and reading clubs are all ways that the library can become a great place to hang out for teens.

Once you've covered the waterfront in terms of various user groups in your community, it makes sense to prioritize those you want to reach because this will determine the level of effort you extend to each one. For example, if your community has a lot of economically disadvantaged children, you might decide that during the course of the next several years you will focus on extending service to this group as a top priority. If, on the other hand, you feel that you are currently providing good service to all groups, but one is especially demanding (the business community, perhaps), you might decide you will give extra weight to serving this group even better.

Over the course of time, as you identify and meet the needs of the groups you've singled out, you can begin to put service to those groups in the middle or near the bottom of your future list of user group priorities. Having established better service to these particular groups, you can now work simply to maintain it while you work to serve other users better.

I have seen this kind of prioritization of service really work for one small library in a neighboring state. Many years ago when, on a camping trip, I met a fellow librarian who told me she had just taken a job as director of a small but active public library. She had been appalled to learn when she applied for the job that although this was a "family" community, the town library had no children's room or children's area. There was a small bin of picture books and that was all.

It's hard to believe that parents in the town didn't object strenuously but apparently the library board and most of the users were of retirement age and, after all, it had always been done that way! The library had always been thought of as a place to get books for leisure reading, and that only. This librarian decided that the library was missing an important opportunity to serve a large (and growing) segment of the community. She convinced her trustees, with the help of a parents' group she activated, to put all other aspects of their service on low-level maintenance while she worked hard to convert an alcove of the building to a children's area.

We've kept in touch over the years and she has since put other priorities at the top of her list. Right now, for example, her library is in the process of building an addition. Apparently, library circulation has nearly tripled over the past decade. She attributes the remarkable increase in library use to children and their parents who have turned what was a quiet reading room into an active community center.

THE COLLECTION

Use of the library's collection will tell you a lot about how your library is used, who is using it, and where your strengths and weaknesses in meeting patron needs lie. As you look at the collection, you should be trying to determine what the most successful aspects are. What formats get the heaviest use? What areas are underused? Where do you get repeated compliments? Are certain areas more prone than others to criticism by your patrons for lack of breadth and depth?

A close look at circulation breakdown and your staff's own empirical observations will tell you if you have heavy use of fiction (perhaps with many mystery readers), if your children's collection is highly used, and if you have a high circulation of popular nonfiction such as cookbooks, parenting, or crafts. Perhaps, biographies are getting the most attention. You will find, of course, that a wide variety of books and materials are circulated, but a pattern of hot spots will develop as well.

It is important to know how your collection is being used because this information will influence your plans to focus on various user groups. If you have low use of your children's collection, for example, it might be a good clue to you that there are underserved portions of your community and you need to make an extra attempt to reach them; on the other hand, it might reinforce your feelings that in your (predominantly retirement age) community, children's services are not in high demand.

HOURS OF OPERATION

Libraries are veritable treasure chests—yielding infinite ways to delight and inform. It's important that as we develop wonderful programs, collections and services we work equally hard to ensure that the treasure chest is open as much as possible to maximize the value of our resources. And it's not just a matter of how many hours you are open, but when you are open as well. As valuable as all of the library's books and materials are, they are of limited value if the public can't get to them when they need to.

It's easy to get comfortable with your hours of operation. You may have had the same hours for years and few have complained. You may be reluctant to change them or add to them because you know that altering schedules will cause some discontent among the staff. Your hours may indeed be fine or they may be failing to meet the needs of a significant portion of your public. It is good to find out.

There are various ways to determine how effective your hours of operation are. First, be objective yourself. Are you open in the evenings at all? How about Sundays? Time is at a premium in our lives today and as more families operate with two working parents, it's important to take a fresh look at those "traditional" hours. Weekends are becoming family time so Sundays could well become your busiest day of the week. What about Saturdays? Are you closing at noon on Saturdays and kicking a good number of people out to do it? In many states, being open at least some evenings and weekends is required in order to meet the state's minimum standards for public libraries. Pay attention to traffic flow. Are people lined up at your door when you open in the afternoon? In all likelihood, if you're honest with yourself, you'll know if your library is closed when many are seeking your service.

SURVEYS

Another good way to find out if your hours are sufficient is by polling your users. Be aware that if you ask simply, "should we be open more?" the answer will probably always be affirmative. The average person (if unaware of the attendant costs) would favor 24-hour-a-day service. Why not? It is better to ask such questions as, "What days and times of the week do you most often use the library?" and "What days and times have you wished to use the library but found it closed?" And, finally, "Knowing that time equals taxpayers' money, would you favor additional library hours and, if so, when would they be?" A very brief survey with two or three quick questions can be completed over the course of a month. If there is consistency in requests for additional hours, you know that you are probably missing an opportunity to serve the community better.

Of course, it also makes sense to find out whether people who *don't* use the library are failing to do so because it's not open at an opportune time for them. Surveying nonusers is a valuable but much more time-consuming project. Users come to you and are probably happy to render their opinions. You must *go* to nonusers, on the other hand, and they may not be as comfortable about giving their opinions. They might feel embarrassed and stigmatized if they confess to not using the library. If you give them a comfortable reason for their nonuse, they are likely to use it whether it is really true or not. For example, if you call someone and ask if they ever use the library and get "no" for an answer and then ask, "Is it because the hours are inconvenient?" they may answer "yes" simply to get out of the conversation or because they don't want to admit they don't read.

If you decide you do want to survey nonusers, plan for the survey very carefully. A personal contact survey may be the best approach for a small community. This can be done either by phone or by arming a group of volunteers with clipboards and dispatching them to places where lots of people gather—the grocery store or the mall for example.

The benefit of the phone survey is that it may be easier to get volunteers to agree to help. They can do this from home and on their own time. The downside is that telemarketers have pretty much soured most of us on engaging with *anyone* we don't know over the phone. If you do decide on a phone survey, be sure that your volunteers know that they should identify themselves immediately by name and let the recipient of the call know that they are taking a very brief survey on behalf of the community's public library. The rule of thumb is that you will probably be able to reach about 50 percent of the people on your list so you may want to try calling about 30 percent of the people in your community to get a final sampling of 15 percent. To get a random sampling, use your local phone book. Determine the number of calls needed for 30 percent and distribute those calls randomly throughout the entire book. Be sure that those selected are residents of your community, then divide the list among your group of volunteers.

A more acceptable approach to many citizens might be to get out into the community with a clipboard and a very brief survey. By going where community members gather, you will find many who are willing to answer a few questions. The downside to this approach in my experience is that it can be harder to get committed volunteers to help. It may be, however, that you can get a good sampling with fewer volunteers working just a couple of Saturdays. A caveat—be sure that you go where people are likely to be in a leisure mode. You don't want to go to the bank over a lunch hour, for example, when people are pressed for time and trying to take care of their own personal business.

It is important that the volunteers you employ are well-trained. Look for ways to elicit information in a respectful way. A good approach to find out why certain people aren't using the library would be to ask, "Have you used the library in the last two months?" If you get a negative response, the follow-up question could be, "Which of these reasons best apply: (a) you had no need for library service, (b) the hours weren't convenient, (c) you've been away or too busy over the last two months."

Phrasing your question in this manner is a sensitive way to find out why - someone doesn't use the library. You can briefly follow up on responses by asking, "Which of the following did you know that the library provides: (a) children's books, (b) videos, (c) reference service by phone, (d) best sellers, (e) local and national newspapers, (f) a wide variety of magazines, (g) parenting books, (h) how-to books?"

The response to this list will tell you just how aware the public is of the various services you offer. In addition, reciting the list is a good way to promote your diversity of service to a nonuser!

Responses will let you know if your hours are working as a barrier to access for some people in your community. You should follow up a response citing hours as a reason for not using the library with a question like, "What would be the three best days and times for you to be able to get to the library?" This information, combined with the information you get from your users, should give you a fairly clear picture of the effectiveness of your current hours and how they might be changed or extended to improve service.

STAFF AND SCHEDULE

Closely linked to hours is the question of staff structure and schedule. Given that your staff is the library's most valuable asset (especially in terms of service) it is crucial for you to determine that every member of the staff is being used to their utmost potential. Be sure that your staff is scheduled so that the workflow is steady and that sufficient staff members are available to meet patrons' needs at all time.

Your own observation might be your best tool in determining if your staff is adequate and adequately scheduled. Take time to get a close look at every phase of your library's operation. Are books ordered on a timely basis, or do hard copies of best sellers finally arrive at the same time they appear in paperback at the local drug store? When books do arrive, do they make it onto the shelves within a week, or do they spend several weeks in the back room waiting to be cataloged or covered? Are there times of the week when patrons are lined up at the front desk while one frantic clerk tries to wait on them (and answer the phone, too)? Is there always a qualified librarian to handle reference questions and advise readers when the library is open?

Be honest in answering these questions. I know it's not easy to admit that you've been remiss in ordering books in a timely manner but don't rationalize; here's a real opportunity to improve. If you are objective in your observations, you will begin to see if you need to reschedule, reassign or increase staff. It might be tempting for you to make the immediate assessment that you need more staff. Whether it's true or not, claiming this to be the case could be (in reality) a way of enabling you to dismiss the entire problem because you have no additional funds. (Go back and reread Chapter One "Creating a Political Base.") It could be that you have sufficient staff; they just need reassignment to tasks that better suit them.

THE BUDGET

Your budget is the best tool you have for accomplishing your goals. I know it's true that there is never enough money and we should always be making the case for the funds we need to accomplish our goals. The investment the public makes in our services is miniscule especially in light of the fact that we are so well used by so many in the community. Funding for libraries should be looked at as an investment in literacy and self-improvement.

Through the planning process, you have an opportunity to analyze your budget as well as your spending patterns. Look over your budgets and expenditures for the last several years so that you can get a firm grip on where your money has traditionally been budgeted and spent. Don't be constrained by past spending patterns in the planning process, however. By designing services from the ground up you might find more creative uses for the money you do receive, and by developing new program concepts, you may have a new and more powerful case to make to your funders. You can share with them the programs you know would be important for your community as well as what they will cost. This is almost always more effective than simply asking for a certain increase to cover the cost of doing business. In getting to an ideal budget, you should consider what you should be offering, how you would best deliver services in a perfect world, and what new opportunities there are for service. As your planning and goal-setting unfolds, you can begin to work towards increasing various portions of your budget or reassigning money to line items that will better serve your stated mission.

Putting It All Together

Once you have completed an environmental scan and have gathered all the information about what you offer and how successfully you've delivered that service, it's time to create a committee to evaluate current service and make recommendations for the future. Include staff, perhaps a member of the Friends group, a trustee (if one is willing) and a couple of interested library patrons. A diverse group of people will offer a variety of perspectives but I recommend keeping this group small and manageable—a core of no more than ten people would be ideal. Too large a group can rapidly become unwieldy and nonproductive.

In order to get the benefit of more input, this core group can set up focus groups in the community to get the widest possible range of ideas for future services. Focus groups should be fairly small, approximately 10 to 15 members, and everyone should be encouraged to speak and brainstorm. It is often very effective to create different "kinds" of focus groups. For example, a focus group of teens, one of parents, one of business leaders, and one of retired people will likely get you both new ideas and a variety of perspectives. I especially enjoyed a focus group of young children in helping design services for children at a previous library. What the kids told us was that they would like a petting zoo, a swimming pool, and an interior playground. What we understood from that was that they were looking for a very interactive, tactile environment. This had a significant impact on our design and services and we think these five to seven year olds really helped us improve our services to them.

When you hold a focus group, be sure that you come prepared with a list of open-ended questions designed to generate a lot of discussion. Start out with general questions such as "Where do you go to get information?" Don't settle for a single answer. It's likely that since this is a library focus group, the members will say simply, "the library." Follow up by asking where else they get information and why. What is more desirable about one source than another? Finding this out will help you replicate what works in the delivery of your own services. Once you've broken the ice and got the group going, you can begin to ask more narrowly focused questions such as "What experience (pleasant or unpleasant) have you had at the library?" and "What could the library do to encourage you to use it more?" "When I say the word 'library,' what feelings does it evoke in you?"

In order to get the most frank and honest answers possible, you may want to have a volunteer or Friend lead the group without library staff present. Since most people have, on the whole, very warm feelings about the library and the staff, they may be loath to say anything negative when staff members are present and, truly, it is usually the unfavorable criticism we get that is most revealing and best helps us to improve. In addition to a volunteer leading the group and asking the questions, you should have another volunteer taking very detailed notes. These notes should be shared in their totality and the note-taker should also be encouraged to write an executive summary that includes their perspective and that of the group leader. For example, the notes themselves might not reveal that there was a lot of energy around the idea of books by mail, or that people were adamant about the fact that your phone service is not very polite. These human interpretations are important.

Based on information collected in the preplanning stage and in the focus groups, the core group should determine where the attention of library service should be centered over the next few years. This will help you decide if you want to enhance service to young children, teens, the elderly community, the homebound, the business community, the information seeker, the fiction reader, or other identifiable client. Of course, you will be doing your best to serve all people, but given the inevitably limited resources (space, time and money), you need to decide what to emphasize during this particular planning period.

THE VISION

Looking to the future, knowing what is on the horizon for library services (or imagining what will be) and looking at what seems to be surfacing as most critical to your users, you and your core group, along with the entire staff, should articulate a vision for your library. This is really just a technique to get you to imagine the future and focus your planning efforts towards achieving that vision. Coming up with the vision should be an organic process. Perhaps it will surface from a focus group of staff and core library supporters. What will your library look like ten years from now? What role will it play in the community? What will make it both critical and unique to the community?

A vision statement should be broad enough to capture a wide concept and allow for continual flexibility in its achievement. For example, a vision statement might be that your library will be the leading provider in individual learning opportunities, and first to capitalize on evolving information technology while retaining the traditional values of personal service to people of all ages. This vision statement implies that the library will be cutting-edge. Perhaps it sees a critical role in "testing" or "piloting" new information technology as valuable to patrons in its own right. If the library, using the collective financial resources of the community, is first or nearly first to use new technology then it gives the public a chance to observe its viability before investing in it personally. Having this as a vision would certainly give you a case for funding. The vision also says that while you will be out there on the leading edge of technology, you will always retain the traditional values that our patrons do love and appreciate. Whatever your vision, it's purpose is to provide direction and focus as you move forward with both the design and implementation of the plan.

THE MISSION

Using the results of the surveys, your committee's input, the focus groups, use and spending trends, and your own judgment, you should now draft a formal mission statement for your library. In all probability, you already have a mission statement, but this should be updated. What might have been a somewhat passive statement about collecting, preserving and disseminating might give way to a more active statement that reflects a desire to reach out and promote the library and its services. Here's an example of one mission statement that shows the library's conception of its services and how it sees itself:

> The Smith Public Library collects and makes available to all members of the community resources that enhance and contribute to individual knowledge, enlightenment and enjoyment. The library especially serves as a place for children to discover the joy of reading and the value of libraries. The library promotes its collection and services so that everyone in the community is aware of its resources and their entitlement to them.

Once you have drafted and accepted a formal "Statement of Mission," all the goals and objectives you set for service should be in response to that mission and under the umbrella of the vision. Looking at the example above, it seems clear that this library will provide materials and service that enable members of the community to engage in individual learning and get information.

While stating in the first sentence that all members of the community are included in the library's mission for service, the Smith Public Library singles out children in its statement for special attention. It is clear that the library accepts responsibility for helping to instill in children a love of reading and a respect for libraries (altruistic *and* self-serving—those children will grow up to be voting members of the community someday).

Finally, work to make sure that the library gets plenty of good press so that people who would benefit by library services are aware of what the library can provide for them.

THE GOALS

Once you have agreed upon a mission statement based on the vision you have for your future services, it is time to set concrete goals and objectives. What do you want to accomplish over the next three to five years? If you have decided that the three major areas you wish to focus on are (1) providing patrons with the materials and resources they need for independent learning, (2) proactive library service to children, and (3) library promotion, then these are the areas to single out when setting goals.

The setting of goals comes before objectives. Since goals reflect the big picture, they will state in broad terms what the library will work toward during the next three to five years. If the first priority is to serve patrons' needs for information, then a logical goal might be: "Members of the community will be able to use the library to get the information they require for independent learning." A second goal for service might be (as in the Smith mission statement above) to increase library use by children. In this case, a goal could be stated as, "The library will identify and respond to the needs of area children." Finally, in keeping with the Smith model, the library has stated that it will actively promote library services. To this end, a goal could be set: "The library will work to ensure that the services it provides have high visibility in the community."

THE STRATEGIES—
WHERE THE RUBBER MEETS THE ROAD

Once you have established your goals for service, it will be much easier (and much more fun) to think about what activities would support implementation of these goals—the strategies you'll use to accomplish them. Now's the time for some real creative thinking. What are you doing now to meet your goals? Are there new opportunities? What did you learn from your patrons and from the focus groups? Be crazy. What audacious things can you do to improve services? What services are no longer necessary? No idea should be off the table in the early stages.

When you've begun to isolate a variety of strategies you can use to improve services, you will have to begin to consider the realistic ways in which they can be implemented. There may be better ways of managing processes to save money or you may have come up with some service ideas that will simply replace older services no longer needed or valued. There will be, however, a variety of cost considerations you'll need to keep in mind as you design concrete plans for implementation.

As we all know, cost considerations go beyond the actual dollar outlay. New ideas often mean additional staff time (including, perhaps, training) as well as some less obvious costs that may have been overlooked in the planning stage. These include supplies, publicity materials, utilities (especially if you are talking about additional hours), replacement or additional copy costs (if you are successful in significantly increasing demand) and the cost of maintaining new or enhanced services if they prove successful.

Another hidden cost can be staff morale. Take into consideration the amount of effort it will cost each applicable staff member to make your plan a success. Plans, no matter how unique or innovative, should be realistic in light of the personnel resources available to you. Even if you envision a new service to be entirely staffed with volunteers, you should realize that volunteers need training, are not always dependable, and they present the same turnover problems as other staff members (perhaps even more so).

I attended a workshop several years ago where this story regarding staff morale was related. A new children's librarian was hired in a small library where previously all children's services (minimal as they were) were provided by volunteers. Hiring a children's librarian was a big step for this library and one that was widely applauded by staff, volunteers and the community alike.

The new children's librarian (I'll call him Mike) was understandably excited about having what amounted to a blank slate to work with. He felt that any innovative programs he implemented would be a success (given that there were only very basic services before). Without consulting the past children's volunteers or members of the library's support staff, Mike immediately scheduled a wide variety of programs and turned in a huge bulk order for the collection that had been neglected over the years.

The programs Mike started, along with the books and materials he ordered, were needed and appreciated by all who frequented the children's room. Staff and volunteers, however, launched a not so subtle anti–Mike campaign. The volunteers who had worked hard over the years to provide basic programming to children felt slighted and even insulted that Mike not only disregarded them in his plans but failed to give them any recognition for past service. The staff felt that Mike should have talked with them about the traditional ordering and materials processing procedure. When his cartons of books arrived the support staff was overwhelmed. Their entire workload was backed up and the enthusiastic (but insensitive) Mike asked daily why the books were taking so long to be processed.

Communication was lacking. Mike should have talked with the staff and volunteers before making any plans. They could have helped him work out a phase-in period for the materials he wanted to order so that their workload wouldn't become unmanageable. The volunteers would have been able to give Mike the benefit of their experience—tips for finding the best program times and an understanding of what age groups used the library most, for example. In addition, the volunteers might have been enlisted to help with the programs, saving Mike some of his valuable time and endearing him to the volunteers as well.

Lack of communication continued to be the problem when the staff and volunteers failed to confront Mike with their feelings. Mike wasn't a bad person, just an overly enthusiastic one. Had he slowed down long enough to work *with* staff and volunteers instead of *around* them, his entry into the new position might have given a boost to staff morale instead of lowering it substantially.

The costs (both hidden and overt) of your strategies will impact their development, but those costs shouldn't limit you. The real key to managing the staff costs in terms of morale is to include staff all along the way. Planning should be fun and create a renewed sense of energy and purpose for everyone. Your job as director is to be both coach and cheerleader. Let your staff know from the beginning that you are working with a blank slate and anything is possible. That's an exciting concept and it should lead the way. "If you can dream it, you can achieve it" should be the staff motto.

Keep in mind that achieving your goals usually makes the effort to get needed additional funding into the budget worthwhile. In fact, your dedication to achieving those goals can help you make a more effective financial case to your town administration. If you are, because of cost, forever avoiding opportunities to deliver a new service or to enhance current service, you are failing to do what your planning information said you should. An important part of your job as director is to recognize new opportunities and to work to take advantage of them.

FOR EXAMPLE, GOAL NUMBER ONE

Let's look at goal number one: "Members of the community will be able to use the library to get the information they require for independent learning." How will you and your staff ensure that members of the community will be successful in using the library as a resource center? You have to break down the services that relate to this goal. You must look at the situation as it exists and at how it could change to improve patron satisfaction.

To facilitate the delivery of information you need to look at both your collection and your staff. You should also be looking at adjunct services such as interlibrary loan, remote reference services (phone, fax, email), and online databases and the Internet. Essentially, you are looking at what the library can (and does) provide in-house and what is available beyond the library's walls.

Because delivery of information services was singled out in the mission statement, it can be assumed that in the preplanning stage, this was identified as an area needing focus. In the preplanning stage you have articulated what your current service looks like and you should have a pretty good idea of why it needs improvement.

If you have found that your nonfiction and reference collections are underused, you should state what you will do to change that based on what in those collections is still viable in light of the availability of online resources.

Strategies might include:

During the first year (insert date):
(1) The assistant librarian will conduct a study of nonfiction circulation statistics to identify areas of little use.
(2) The library director and the children's librarian will review whether low use might be a result of insufficient materials in identified areas or availability of alternative resources such as those available online.
(3) The library director and the children's librarian will ensure that their respective collections are fully weeded to eliminate out-of-date materials, make the useful materials more visible, and identify areas in the collections that need improvement.
(4) The library director will ensure that a log is kept of all reference and research questions brought to the library, when they are brought or called in, and how successful the library was in answering them.
(5) The library director will work with the assistant librarian to analyze online resources and make recommendations for purchase of services along with necessary upgrades for hardware and software.
(6) The library director will meet with all desk volunteers and clerks on three separate occasions to emphasize the importance of referring queries to a qualified librarian.
(7) The assistant librarian will keep a detailed log of all interlibrary loan requests

originating at this library to determine if there is a pattern of subjects and titles frequently requested.

In this case, the strategies for the first year involve the completion of a detailed analysis of the collection and use of online resources and the nature of reference service at your library. By the end of this year, you will have a much better understanding of exactly where your weaknesses lie and you can then work, in the second year, to address those weaknesses. The next set of objectives relating to goal number one might look something like this:

During the second year (insert date):
(1) The library director and the children's librarian will purchase up to date materials for those portions of their collections that have been found to be inadequate or out-of-date during the weeding and collection evaluation period.
(2) The library director will evaluate the reference log to determine when the greatest use of the reference collection occurs and to identify patterns that reflect weaknesses in the reference collection.
(3) The library director will read bibliographies, reviews and other library literature to determine what reference sources would make valuable additions to the collection based on use, and what the cost of these sources will be.
(4) The library director will purchase those identified reference sources that are affordable.
(5) The library director will prepare a case for the reference sources needed (both print and digital) but not purchased so that their cost can be included in the following year's budget.
(6) The library director will evaluate the reference log to identify times of heavy traffic and assign a qualified librarian to assist patrons during these times.
(7) The library director will determine if additional staff is needed to ensure that a qualified librarian is readily available to render user assistance at all times when the library is open and prepare a case for additional staff, if needed.
(8) The assistant librarian will analyze trends in email reference and make recommendations for promoting this service and managing increased use along with recommendations for turnaround time in response.
(9) The assistant librarian will develop a file of local agencies and organizations and what services they provide so that the library is able to act as a community resource center.

For the following year or two, continue to spell out objectives to accomplish your goals. The objectives in this case would include refining online services both as a customer service and as collection development. The final year in this planning period should include both evaluation and a report to the trustees on the success of accomplishing the set goals.

The strategies you set need to be specific. You must not only state what will be done to accomplish a certain goal, but spell out who will do it, when it will be done and, finally, how the success of your efforts will be measured. In the example above, a time line has been set out. Because serving the informational needs of patrons is largely a professional task, the strategies in this case fall either to the library director, the children's librarian, or the assistant librarian. They, of course, might delegate some of the work involved in meeting the objectives, but in the end, they are responsible for them.

Remember that these strategies are set to accomplish goal number one only. The children's librarian will only be called on here to evaluate the use and currency of her own collection. Because goal number two will be focusing on children's services, it is realistic to assume she will be busy accomplishing another set of objectives as well.

Finally, both goals one and two will be achieved in concert with goal number three, which deals with library promotion. In fact, the success of the first two goals depends significantly on the success of the third.

Setting goals and developing strategies for their implementation is the best way to ensure that the service you are providing is the best possible. Setting goals and refining strategies does, however, require time and commitment from your staff and trustees (especially if it means getting additional revenue). Keeping this in mind, the goals you set for each planning period should not exceed realistic expectations for success and they should be developed in a way that shares the workload as effectively as possible among your staff.

MEASURING SUCCESS

Setting goals and working on strategies without providing some criteria for evaluation would be like sending all your good work and intentions down a black hole. How will you know if what you are doing is meaningful? In addition, without continual evaluation, its difficult if not impossible to make changes in your approach—to constantly tweak the implementation so that the library can continually improve. In the case above, examination of circulation statistics and a reference log will show if use is increasing and if your success in meeting your patrons' needs is improving. Weeding the collection will ensure that the materials available are meaningful and up to date.

Not all of your assessments will (or should) be quantifiable, however. Take interlibrary loan use for instance. Judging the success of your library's ability to work well as a community learning and resource center by examining interlibrary loan transactions could be misleading. For example, if you have been successful in encouraging greater use of the library (and the strategies for doing so would fall under goal number three), then you might find that your interlibrary loan traffic increases as well. On the other hand, if you have failed to respond to frequent requests by purchasing more of your own materials in popular areas, then you might judge your efforts in this regard to have failed. There is a degree of professional judgment that needs to apply to interpretation of results, but be careful not to confuse this with rationalization!

While the study and use of data such as circulation statistics are good ways to determine your success in serving your community, they are not the only ways. They should be used in careful combination with a variety of other factors such as community profile and type of library use. If your town is losing population, it is likely that circulation will drop or remain stable. If you are successful in providing excellent online services, use of your nonfiction print collections could drop as could use of print reference sources. If employment opportunities are changing, that could well change the nature of the informational services you provide, and that change might not be reflected in the statistics. The reference log will give you a better look at how well you are answering questions, the formats used for both asking questions (remote or in-house) and answering them, and whether your performance is improving. Similarly, your work to improve the collection itself necessarily means that patrons will have access to better information and sources of education.

Patron Satisfaction

Planning is an effective way to identify and improve the service you give, but how you operate on a daily basis in meeting the needs of your patrons may be more a matter of policy and practice than of planning. How do you ensure that when a patron leaves your library she is satisfied that her needs have been met?

It is not possible for public libraries (especially small public libraries) to ensure that every request a patron makes will be met successfully at the time it is requested. You can, however, ensure that "basic" material *is* always available at your library and you can take advantage of a variety of opportunities to get initially unavailable material or information to your patron in a timely way.

First of all, what is "basic"? This may vary with each library depending on patron or community profile, but "basic material" would typically include résumé guides, medical encyclopedias, addresses for major corporations and businesses, college guides and local college catalogs, and government guides listing state and national politicians and leaders. You can be sure this information is always available by keeping copies of it in the noncirculating reference collection and creating a folder for relevant online sites.

Many of the books you might reserve for reference will also be available in the circulating collection, but you do want to be sure that you can immediately give a patron such basic information as that contained in *The Occupational Outlook Handbook*, for example. You can stretch your budget by putting an older edition of a given source into circulation when you update the work for your reference collection.

Interlibrary loan is another way to get information you don't have on hand to a patron. Of course the obvious drawback to this approach is time. With electronic mail and online databases, however, the time a patron must wait is becoming shorter and shorter. You might also be able to utilize another local library. Could this information be found in the hospital's library, the school's library, at the local history museum? If the information a patron needs is of the "quick answer" variety, why not make a call to the state library's reference department? Getting the information the patron needs to them as soon as you can is an important component of good library service.

As for popular reading material, we all know that slight feeling of dread that comes with the publishing of another best seller by a popular writer. You know that you will have to spend precious dollars on extra copies. Given the expected demand (and the high cost of best sellers), how do you draw the line on the number of extra copies you buy?

There is a theory that advocates buying enough copies of a title to eliminate a waiting list altogether (see Chapter Three). No matter how successful you are in obtaining a fair budget for your library, however, you will never have enough money to buy all the copies of the latest best seller you need to ensure that no one has to wait *and* to be able to buy everything else you feel the library should have. If you decide that meeting the immediate needs of best-seller readers is of primary importance, you will have to do so at the expense of other library users.

According to proponents of the no-waiting-list book ordering approach, in meeting the needs of this demanding clientele you will not only be doing a good job of providing service, but you will be endearing a large segment of library users to your cause. This happy group, so goes the theory, will rise to your defense in times of budget crisis. To a degree this is probably true, but I believe that in hard times, even they take a good look at what is dispensable and have second thoughts about committing a burgeoning tax burden to multiple copies of Danielle Steel and Tom Clancy.

Happily, there are ways to satisfy the voracious demands of your best-seller readers without going broke. Consider implementing a "Seven Day Book" plan where the hottest best sellers on reserve can only be checked out for a week. Those who read these books usually read them quickly and this will create a much higher turnover rate for these titles, dramatically lowering the number of copies you need to vanquish a long list of reserves. If you do implement something like this, be prepared for an initial outcry among your users. They will worry that they won't be able to get all the books they want at one time and get them read and back to you. They're right. They may have to take fewer books at a time (or fewer best sellers). They'll soon discover something else, however, and that is that they are getting the books they reserved much more quickly. Since reduced loan periods for best sellers have worked so well in so many libraries, you should give it serious consideration. Perhaps you can let your patrons know that you are trying it as a pilot project for one year and that you'll get feedback for a permanent decision at the end of the trial. Usually, when the year is over, the patrons are well accustomed to the change, appreciate getting the books more quickly, and like the fact that the budget can now be stretched further.

In the end it's important that the budget is spent on meeting the broadest range of needs within your community. This is not just an important service issue, it's a values issue as well. I would rather gamble my future on something a little less ephemeral than best sellers. I want to be sure that people who need information on how to improve any aspect of their lives get it at the public library. I want to be sure that if a patron wishes to continue her education independently she can do so at the public library. I want to be sure that if a child develops a new interest in knights and armor, she can indulge that interest at the public library. Ultimately, people should remember how they began to confront their past history of childhood abuse or how their children got turned on to books or how they learned about increasing the retail value of their home—all at the public library.

There's no doubt that loaning best sellers is a staple of our service. But, is it the most important thing we do? Because we live in a world of finite resources, we have to face the fact that for every book we select, there are others we can't. Rather than spending disproportionately high sums to vanquish a waiting list, you might work harder on developing plans to circulate these books more quickly and suggesting interesting alternatives until the patron's name is up. By suggesting alternatives, you are providing that "value-added" service that libraries are known for and it is likely that you will turn readers on to new authors they might never have discovered on their own.

Quality of Service: The Intangibles

What you deliver in the way of service is tangible. You can list these services, modify them, and evaluate them in an objective way. As important as the "what" you provide your patrons, however, is the "how." The quality of the services you provide is inextricably linked to the *way* in which you provide them.

In speaking to a group of librarians, John Kenneth Galbraith once stated his belief that the service provided by public libraries could never truly be replicated in the private sector. He talked not only about cost-effectiveness (which is probably what we do best), but about attitudes and commitment. Although we as a profession sometimes suffer from an image that suggests librarians are mean-spirited and antisocial, I find I agree with Galbraith that, for the most part, those of us offering library service to the public are committed to serving well. Our motivation comes from this desire and it means that our decision-making regarding service will be based on what's best for the patron not what will garner the highest profit—they are not always the same thing.

As committed as we are, however, I believe that we are also extremely vulnerable to complacency. We have a responsibility to evaluate the quality of our service because the public, for the most part, does not know good library service from bad. If you think this a gross exaggeration, consider how many times you've been asked what it is, exactly, that you do, with the implication that all you *really* do is sit around and read. Similarly, remember the common belief that all we librarians do is check out books. If the public is unaware of what we do, how are they to evaluate how well we're doing it? In reality, they probably can't, or at least they can't as well as we can. Our responsibility for honest and critical self-evaluation is one we must accept as part of our commitment to delivering quality service.

ATTITUDES

The best building, collections, and programs in the world will not make up for poor public service by your staff. Though collections and programs are our tools of the trade, and library buildings help us to house and deliver these assets, what we really offer is service. It's service that distinguishes us from bookstores and book warehouses. It's our ability to add significant value to our "tools" that make public libraries so special. It is critically important, then, that we provide this service in an extremely customer-friendly way.

It would be difficult to list objectives that support the goal of pleasant, friendly service. I'm not sure I would want to see the smile of the clerk who is following the requirement that she smile at least ten times during the course of her shift! While you might not be able to mandate happiness, you can certainly insist on pleasant service both in person and over the phone. Obviously as director, you want to create an environment that fosters commitment to good service and produces employees who feel comfortable in their positions and who know they have the power to make the work they do even better. You should set the example yourself by treating your staff with the same courtesy and respect that you want them to show the patrons. It's also important to talk about good customer service on a regular basis with your staff so they understand that it's an integral part of the organizational culture and not optional.

Friendly, courteous service should not be simply a goal, but the only acceptable manner of behavior when dealing with the public. Attitudes might not be objectifiable but the behaviors that emanate from attitude are. Developing courteous, helpful behavior is something you can and should do.

BEHAVIOR

The manner in which patrons (and fellow workers) are treated is an area you can control by setting guidelines for behavior and requiring that all employees follow them. For example, I consider pointing to be a capital offense. Any patron who's had the gumption to come to the desk for help *always* deserves more than a finger launched in some obscure direction with a terse, "It's over there on the second shelf, you can't miss it." Anyone asking where to find a particular item is entitled to very clear instructions on where to find it. Better yet, if there is not a line of anxious patrons behind her, you might escort her to the material. In a small library you can do that; it's one of the things that makes our service special.

Another one of the worst ways to treat a patron is answering her query on, say, dogs with "Just look under 'Dogs' in the online catalog." Think about it. This is a library, and anyone who knows how to use the library would already know to look under "Dogs" in the catalog. Obviously, *this* person doesn't know how to use the library, doesn't know where the online catalog is, or doesn't need general information on dogs. It is very possible that this patron may, in reality, want to know who in the area breeds them. Staff should be trained to follow a reference question with a question of their own to ensure they know for sure what information is actually needed.

If volunteers or clerks are unsure of handling a question, they should *always* respond to the patron with, "Just one moment, please, I'll get someone who can help you find the information you're looking for."

You might not be able to force a charming lilt into the voices of all your staff and volunteers, but you can insist that they use common courtesy at all times. This should include telephone manners too. We've probably all been greeted with "Hellos" that are easily interpreted as "what the hell do *you* want?" Not a pleasant experience. Simply adding "May I help you?" on the end of a hello can go a long way. I believe strongly that friendly service is very important. Surveys have shown repeatedly that poor attitudes on the part of library personnel can create barriers to access. It makes sense when you think about it. Public libraries may have a monopoly on fee-free information and recreational reading services, but that alone may not be enough to draw in the patron who feels that she will be treated rudely.

Reference Service

It is not enough that we make information available to the public: we must also help them use it. As the digital divide closes, this will be more important than ever. It's the "service" component of information delivery that makes libraries valuable— this has been true in the past and it's even truer in the Information Age. Reference and reader assistance is, I must confess, my favorite part of librarianship. I'd like to point to altruistic motives here—the joy of helping others find what they need and thereby making some small contribution to their well-being. Truly, that's part of it. The larger part, however, is that providing good reference service makes me seem so smart! How gratifying it is to respond quickly and efficiently to a patron's request for information she isn't sure even exists.

Answering a patron's question in a timely and accurate way involves not only knowing the collection and understanding the world of online information, it also means knowing people and how to work well with them. As anyone who has done reference work will attest, many people simply do not know how to ask for the information they really need. It is up to us to conduct a thorough reference interview that involves both tact and savvy. Here are some examples of reference service I've actually witnessed over the years. Put together, they make a pretty good list of how *not* to handle reference questions. Consider, for example, that simple question, "Do you have information on dogs?" Here are some inappropriate responses: (1) "Yes." [Long pause while patron figures out she must follow this question up with another about where to find the information.] (2) "Yes we do, just look under 'dogs' in the catalog." (3) "Yes, the books we have are under 636.7 on the shelves." (4) "Gee, I'm not really sure, but I think so." (5) "Yes we do, they're right over there [pointing] next to that big red book, you can't miss them."

Now be honest: you have probably heard or been the perpetrator of the responses above or those similar to them. The correct way to answer the question is by following with a question of your own so that you can be sure of the exact kind of information the patron needs. You could ask, "Just what kind of information were you looking for?" If the patron was actually looking for local breeders or information on dog training, this should come out at this point. If the patron says she needs just general information, you might want to ask, "Are you interested in a special breed, or would you like information about a variety of breeds?"

The important thing is to engage the patron in enough conversation to elicit from her the true nature of her request. By the same token, certain areas may be more sensitive and require more subtle probing on your part. A patron inquiring about information on herpes, for example, may not want to get into particulars with you. It would not, obviously, be appropriate to follow her question with, "So, are you looking for this information for yourself?" A matter-of-fact and pleasant attitude should increase the patron's comfort and allow you to find out if the patron wants to know about the latest method of treatment or is more interested in the emotional aspects of the virus.

After you've done a good job of walking the patron through the resources you have available, it may be difficult for the patron to say, "But this isn't what I wanted at all." Not wanting to feel ungrateful or burdensome, many patrons will simply leave without getting what they need, even if it's sitting right there on your shelves. So the most fail-safe way to ensure that you have met the patron's needs is to follow up every transaction with, "Does this information answer your question or should we find something more?"

MAXIMIZING YOUR RESOURCES

Here's a flash for you—reference sources are often extremely expensive! One of the great challenges facing directors of small libraries is to provide for the informational needs of their diverse clientele on an extremely limited budget.

There are ways to increase the effectiveness of your current reference collection, both print and electronic. It makes good sense, for example, to develop a reference log if you don't already have one. For about six months to a year, keep detailed entries in this log about what was asked and how (and if) you were able to answer it. You will then be able to use this information to assess the resources you own or subscribe to.

Some indications will be obvious. You may be receiving a lot of requests for information on specific areas of health care that you can't answer. Obviously, you will want to investigate ways to beef up your health reference collection. You may want to contact the area hospital and see if they can provide you with access to some of their databases. It might be possible and affordable for you to be added to their license agreement as just one additional professional user.

Another area sometimes overlooked in answering reference questions is your nonfiction collection. Be sure that you locate reference materials close to this collection. I was told by one library consultant when we were designing an addition to our library that we should put the fiction collection on the first floor near the main desk. The reason given was that the majority of books checked out in public libraries are fiction, and we should make this collection as convenient as possible for the patrons.

I argued against this idea. First of all, it isn't necessarily true that most books checked out from public libraries are fiction. Second, while accessing the fiction collection is fairly simple (books in alphabetical order by author), use of the nonfiction collection often requires assistance. Finally, I pointed out, the nonfiction collection is used heavily by our public services librarian in answering patrons' questions. I remember this consultant answering my objections with, "Oh, so you want to locate the nonfiction on the first floor for *your* convenience?" Of course not. This is definitely a customer service issue. Nonfiction is a useful resource for reference and readers' advisory services. Don't hesitate to use it to get the answers you need. Hopefully it is located in an area that will increase its usefulness to your patrons.

Children's Services

It's hard to imagine that anything could be more fundamental for public libraries than children's services. First, for preschool children, public libraries offer the very first institutional introduction to the world of books and reading. As illiteracy becomes a more and more visible problem in our country, we are beginning to recognize what children's librarians have known all along. That is, if you can turn a young child on to reading, the habit is likely to become a lifelong joy.

As a society we have recognized our collective responsibility to educate our children. Public libraries can and should play a crucial role in that education. Our role may not be as formal as that of the public schools but that makes it no less important. We are lucky because we have the luxury of providing pure delight, no strings attached. No grades, no raising hands, no curricular constraints. We offer a unique opportunity for individual discovery and adventure.

How thrilling is this service we have to offer our children, and how clear their thirst for it! How amazing it is, then, that youth services often take a back seat in the development of library priorities. Many small libraries have no children's librarian at all, and many dedicate only a small fraction of the total book budget to support this service. There are a variety of reasons for a failure to develop excellent children's services and these should be examined honestly and with an open mind.

For one thing, children are less demanding and critical than adults. With a few exceptions (Harry Potter, for example), children won't be rushing in for a specific best-selling title. In addition to that, they are not likely to complain if the material you offer them on, say, space exploration is out of date. Children are also satisfied to read the same books over and over again. In short, they are easily pleased—and thus easily overlooked. Even parents are often easily satisfied. While some parents may object to second-class service for children, it's probable that most other parents will be grateful for any children's library at all.

It is precisely because we can get away with cutting corners in the children's room that our obligation *not* to do so is strong. In children's services more than in any other aspect of library services we must be our own best critics.

Second, children have no clout. They don't vote, they don't call their town government, they don't write letters to the editor when the library budget is threatened. In addition, some of us may feel that if we are primarily perceived as a place for children, we will lose some of our prestige in the community. This is sad to the degree that it is true.

I understand that service to children does not typically bring with it a high degree of prestige. This only makes the challenge greater. If it is true in your community that children's services are not highly honored, you and your staff should work not only to develop the best children's service you can, but to market that service along with the rest of the wonderful things you do in the most positive, sophisticated way possible.

View this as an opportunity to educate your community. Through your promotional efforts, explain how important reading is to the educational development of children. Talk about the problems of illiteracy in our country and about approaches to eradicating it. Our efforts must be directed not only to teaching the skill of reading to illiterate adults, but to preventing illiteracy in the first place. We do that by opening the world of reading to children. Studies have shown that children exposed early to books are more likely to become good readers. Common sense tells me that children who value libraries will become adults who value libraries. Service to children is important. Let's get that message out both by example and by advocacy on their behalf.

TEENS

It is apparent that we are in the midst of a resurgence in our commitment to providing teenagers with special services geared to meeting their unique needs. Thank heavens. This is such an important group and it is a group that has very special needs. Unfortunately, because the group is small and because many people have difficulty working with them and appreciating these wonderful years of development, they tend to get either overlooked, or cut from the budget when the hard times roll around. It is probably this latter issue that contributed to a loss of young adult librarians over the past several decades and caused many of us delivering library services to downplay services and collections to this special user group.

Happily, teen services are no longer being marginalized in many libraries across the country. Teen centers and spaces are cropping up in even the smallest libraries. Regardless of overall library space, you can and should find a section of your library that you can devote exclusively to teen services. It can be as small as a corner but if it has the right components, it will suffice and be used. Be sure that you make the space jazzy and attractive. You can do this successfully by asking a few of your teens to form a committee for the purpose of outfitting and designing the look of the teen corner. In fact, this group could be the beginning of a new teen advisory committee. See if you can get a local interior designer to volunteer some time to work with this group and give them direction and ideas. Give the group a small budget for furnishings, rugs, poster art, and so on. The Friends might be able to help with finances.

Once you've created an attractive section for teens and have created a teen advisory committee in the process, use these resources to begin to crank up your services to this group. The advisory committee can be prevailed upon to help select books for their collection, to promote library services among their peers, to design programs for younger kids at the library and to form a teen volunteer task force. Consider special programs for teens. Maybe one on designing websites. After this kind of training, you may be able to get a group of teens working on developing a teen site on your own web page and keep it updated.

The more you keep teens engaged, the more they will use the library. Though we don't often think of it this way, this group is often one "at risk" for not continuing the lifelong habit of reading. We should do everything we can to keep them interested in libraries, and we can benefit by their participation in providing advice, assistance, and programs for the library.

EVALUATING YOUTH SERVICES

Because youth services are a critical component of your library's services, you should evaluate the strengths and weaknesses of the service you currently offer. Take a look at your community profile. If your library serves a community that is predominantly of retirement age, you will be justified in dedicating proportionately lower funds to development of youth services. Just keep in mind that even if children and teens are a small part of your town's demographics, they are still entitled to the same level of high-quality service you provide all your patrons.

If your community is like most, however, you will have a good proportion of young people, and your library budget should reflect this. The budget for youth materials should be high enough so that sufficient new books are purchased each year to meet demand. Additionally, there should be enough money available so that replacement copies can be bought on a regular basis (young children, as we all know, can often love a book to destruction). Also, you should seriously consider your staff structure. If half of your patrons are children and you don't have a youth librarian on staff, you are clearly neglecting this large patronage with special needs.

There may not be standards for how many staff hours should be dedicated to youth services based on use, but plain common sense may help you identify weaknesses in this area. If you're truly committed to offering the best youth services possible, you can begin to work with your staff and trustees (along with a few parents who actively use the children's collection) to develop your own standards for service.

In developing these standards, be sure to consider other avenues for enrichment available to children and teens in your community. If there are few opportunities for kids to experience independent learning, intellectual growth and quality reading, your own youth services become automatically more important.

Programs

Fun, creative opportunities, a chance to share ideas with others, good visibility for the library, new patrons—these are some of the rewards of library programming. Fortunately, library programs can be creative and informative without taking a big bite out of the library's budget. By using lots of imagination, volunteers when possible, and local talent, you can sponsor top-notch programs on a shoestring.

Of course, there is *some* cost involved, but it doesn't have to be a lot. Consider, for example, the cost of time. Even if a superior volunteer is taking on a particular program, some of your time (or that of a staff member) will and should be involved. Remember that no matter which individual is directly responsible for the program itself, in the end its success or failure is a direct reflection on you and the library, so you or a member of your staff will want to be in on the planning. This time should always be reimbursed; don't expect a staff member to be involved with planning or to attend a program without compensating them.

Another minor cost to consider is that of publicity. Good publicity is absolutely crucial to the success of your program. No matter how great your speaker or timely your topic, all effort is wasted if there is no audience. This is a lesson that can not be overstressed. You'll understand this if you've ever sat alone with an invited speaker in an empty meeting room while the minutes tick past the appointed hour!

Luckily, some of the most effective avenues open to you for promotion are free (radio, newspaper and in-house newsletter announcements, for example), but you might also want to produce posters and flyers to hang around town. A little ingenuity can make this a slick yet inexpensive operation. Get a talented volunteer or staff member to make them, or try a little clip art. You might also look into inexpensive computer programs specially designed to produce graphics for flyers, posters and banners. Whatever method you use, it's important to be sure that the end product looks good. The flyer or poster you produce is representing the library, so be sure it conveys the image you want the public to see.

You can further reduce your costs in terms of time and publicity by working with other organizations in town to cosponsor programs at the library. For example, in the spring you might want to invite the extension service to speak on garden pests. How about getting in touch with your local history museum to see if they'd like to cosponsor a program on, say, researching family history? Maybe the League of Women Voters in your community would be willing to make arrangements for a candidates' forum if you will provide the space and publicity. The ideas for cooperation are limited only by the number of groups in your community who would like the exposure and opportunity to inform as much as you do.

In addition to tapping the resources of other area organizations, there is probably a wealth of local "celebrities" who might be convinced to give a few hours of their time to the library as a gift. Consider, for example, your mayor or town manager. When was the last time they were offered a forum just for the fun of it to speak on a topic of their own choosing? In addition to providing a good program, inviting these people can have the added benefit of earning you extra brownie points. What about a local crafts person, or the town clerk—now there's a person with stories to tell! The local kindergarten teacher is probably an expert at reading aloud; how about a read-aloud for adults? The more you think about it, the more ideas you will come up with.

Once in a while, you may feel like bringing a big name author or storyteller to your library. I think that's a great idea. The bigger the name, the more publicity you'll receive, and the more likely you are to bring new people into the library. For these programs, get a little help from your Friends. You can sell them on the idea that sponsoring such an event will generate the kind of publicity they've always dreamed about.

You don't have to have celebrities and speakers to have a successful program, however. Reading-discussion groups, for example, have been a staple of library programming since the days of the "Great Books" talks. While it's true that in most states grant money is available to provide both books and speakers for these events, it is also typically true that a substantial amount of money is required of your library first.

The programs provided through grants are terrific, but if you are really strapped for money you can do your own version for a relatively small price. Ask a volunteer to facilitate the discussion, or plan on a play-reading. Then pick an interesting book or two that are out in paperback. By buying in bulk, you should be able to get the books at a pretty good price. Check out the discount rates offered by your vendor on mass market paperbacks and shop around if it isn't that great. You're likely to find discounts of up to 50 percent off if you're buying a title in quantity and this will help with the costs of your program significantly.

When the program is over, you can then recoup some of the money spent on books by either offering to sell the books to interested participants (at your cost of course) or by offering the "program" to another library. If you can sell a neighboring library on the idea, it can buy the books from you. Offer them at a price somewhat less than your own cost since they are used.

CHILDREN'S PROGRAMS

Programs for children have long been a staple of library service and they are a critical component of youth services. Engaging children in the joys of reading and learning is very successfully done through interactive programs. There is no area in which creativity is more obvious and productive than in the variety of children's programs I've heard about. Programs for kids are so important because they help connect books to the world around them. In addition, programs can expand the world for children by introducing them to new cultures, new ideas, and new kinds of literature.

If your library isn't offering a lot of diverse and creative programs for kids, you should discuss some ideas with your children's librarian. In all likelihood, however, children in your community have been treated to everything from the traditional storytime and puppet show to the more avant-garde baseball card swap and cityscape model-making. Nonetheless, don't let the creative energy and expertise already in existence at your library be taken for granted. Your children's librarian is a valuable resource; use her and appreciate her!

You've Got It, Now Promote It!

All your hard work in continually improving library services to your community will be for naught if no one knows about them. Even your most loyal and frequent users might be surprised to learn the full scope of the services you offer. It may come as a complete surprise to a loyal patron that you have a special teen collection, for example, and this user may be a high school teacher or the parent of a teen. Best-seller readers might be thrilled and surprised to learn that you have a reading club that meets to talk about popular books every Wednesday. If you have surprises in store for your regular patrons, imagine what those who don't use your library don't know about it. It's very important that we not only design and deliver excellent services, we have to work hard to make sure that everyone knows about them.

In Chapter One of this book under "Year-Round Advocacy," I have discussed using the newspaper and the broadcast media in a politically savvy way for your library. These same avenues should be used on a regular basis for announcing and talking about the importance of the services you offer. Consider working with your local radio station to develop a set of public service announcements (PSAs) to encourage either the general use (and value) of your library, or to highlight targeted services such as youth services or information services. If you do develop PSAs, be sure to keep them general enough so that they can be played over and over and remain relevant. Specific programs can be announced through your library's newsletter, through flyers, over the radio, and in the newspaper.

Your library's website is another excellent way to both promote your library and to offer services remotely. Be sure that you website is eye-catching, easy to use, and information rich. It may be the first impression of you for many nontraditional library users. If you are not technically savvy or creative enough to design and maintain the website yourself, give serious consideration to assigning this to someone else on staff. It may well mean that you send a staff member (or yourself) to get solid instruction in building a website, but this would be well worth it as skill in this area is fast becoming indispensable for your library. A short-term solution might be to contract the work out, but, let's face it, if your website is to be a dynamic and useful tool, it will have to be updated continuously, so it makes most practical sense to have someone on the library staff looking after it. Furthermore, as a new type of "collection," it will probably have the best development under the direct guidance of a good librarian.

In "Planning" earlier in this chapter, I also talked about nonuser surveys as a way to get the word out about the wide scope of services you offer. In addition, you can partner with other organizations in town to promote your services. This is another excellent way to broaden your reach to those who do not, currently, use your library. Your library has something of value for everyone in the community, and everyone in the community supports the library through taxes, so it's important that you reach as many people as possible in as many ways as possible to show them what you've got—what *they've* got.

Free Versus Fee

No matter how hard I try, I cannot reconcile fees for service with the mission of public libraries. Fees are simply antithetical to our purpose. Both the Library Bill of Rights and the librarian's Code of Ethics (for copies, see Appendices G and H), address the importance of equality of service to our patrons. No matter how you look at it, charging fees abridges that equality because some people have the ability to pay and some don't.

What is at risk when you begin to charge fees (typically for "special" services) is the unique promise of public libraries that no matter who you are, you have the right—and we'll give you the opportunity—to know, to be informed, to learn. Furthermore, this opportunity will be inherently equal to that of every other person in this community. Is this a mission to compromise?

Librarians can be proud of their track record to eliminate barriers to users of public libraries. We have fought for and won the right to keep controversial materials on our shelves. We have gone to great expense to ensure that those with physical handicaps are able to use our facilities. We devote time, energy and financial resources to bringing library services to those who can't come to us. After all this, how can we justify erecting barriers for the poor by charging fees for our services?

Our communities reaffirm their belief in the importance of access every year when they agree to support our services through taxes. Taxes (theoretically at least) are levied in such a way that those who carry the largest financial burden are those best able to do so. The purpose of such a system is to ensure that everyone in the community has the same access to what are considered basic services, such as police protection, road maintenance, public education and *library service*.

As librarians, we put that access in jeopardy every time we ask $1.00 for a video (after all, it's just a buck); charge a small price for a program (just to help cover the costs); ask for postage for interlibrary loan (even if we should have had the material ourselves); or charge for any other kind of "special service." When we do this, we are effectively denying or obstructing service to poor people in our community— ironically the very people who might have the most to gain from our services. Even offering "scholarship" waivers is ineffective (not to mention demeaning). We all know that there are people whose pride will not allow them to ask for a handout.

While I stand firm on the belief that the tax-supported community library should not retax its citizens by assessing additional service fees, I am also a realist. I know the counterarguments and understand their validity. Budgets are small and many services are not adequately supported by the budget. In fact, goes the argument, some services would not be available at all if it weren't for fees.

I do not underestimate the cost of a video collection or the development of a technology infrastructure. I know that postal rates continue to rise and that dealing with interlibrary loan is a time-consuming project. I understand the temptation to recoup costs for programs by charging admission or by passing a hat; I know that programs have been used successfully as fundraisers. These are all realities, but there are other ways to accommodate the costs without turning patrons away from your doors, and of course that's what you do when you charge a fee.

If you find that the need to implement new services or maintain "special" services is not adequately supported by your budget, and that the present budget is not likely to increase, it may be time to take a good look at how you are allocating the money you *do* have. If videos are the budget problem, perhaps a partial solution lies in another collection. Is your periodical collection, for example, broader than it needs to be given that you are already subscribing to full-text databases? Will creating a shorter loan period for best sellers save you some money? Do you need multiple copies of encyclopedias when you have online access for patrons? Constantly watch your traditional spending patterns and make it a habit to ask whether we still really need this. The money you save in one area can be used to meet a costly demand in another.

Prioritize your services to determine where cuts can be made if the new service is more important. I don't believe there is a lot of fat in the budgets of most small public libraries, but sometimes tough choices do have to be made.

Once you've made the tough choices and it's clear that some aspects of your service are underfunded, you must start being a squeaky wheel. Let the public know what services they are forgoing because the budget is inadequate, and let them know what that means for the quality of service they're getting. Remember, it's the *public's* library and they should know and feel some sense of responsibility for what you are *not* providing as well as what you are.

As you work on raising that budget, there are other alternatives to fees. While I am fundamentally opposed to letting the Friends of the Library pick up the tab on expenses that rightfully belong in the operating budget (their money is insecure, and you don't want to set any precedents), they might be prevailed upon to *start* a new service while you work on your campaign to get money to maintain it. For other costly services (such as development of public access computer labs, for example), you might be able to successfully attract grants to cover the costs for wiring, hardware, software and sometimes even staff. Because the digital divide is an issue of keen concern to many foundations and businesses, your pitch to get external support for this service will fall on fertile ground.

Finally, get rid of the notion of "special" service. While I maintain that *all* our service is "special," I feel paradoxically that it is all "basic" as well (if it's not basic, don't waste precious time and money on it). I just can't understand why we let one patron check out $100 worth of best sellers for free and then tell another patron she has to pay $1.00 for one book through interlibrary loan because it is a "special" service. How is that determination made? Are best sellers more important? Or is it that interlibrary loan is such a pain in the neck that, subconsciously, we're trying to discourage it?

Charging fees for service is not only wrong on principle—it is dangerous in practical terms. In addition to creating discriminatory services, it sets an unfortunate precedent. How are we going to explain the difference between "basic" and "special" services to members of our town governments (who will probably be delighted by the idea of fees—until *they* need an online search)? Can we articulate the difference well enough to protect those "basic" services of ours? Where will we draw the line when they ask that other services be supported by fees? These are questions that must be asked (and answered well) every time we charge a fee for "special" library services.

Outreach

There are two basic types of outreach services addressing very different functions. One is to bring the library's services to those who are isolated from your facility by physical, geographical or social barriers. The other kind of outreach encourages greater use of the library in-house by targeted groups and organizations in your community. While service to those who are isolated is ongoing, the outreach efforts aimed at various groups in the community are usually made on a one-time basis.

Reaching out to those who for various reasons face obstacles in coming to the library is an important part of a library's overall service. If the primary focus of good service is to increase access to and utilization of the library's collection, then it is not enough to focus effort only on those patrons who regularly use our facility. If we mean to fairly serve *all* those who are entitled to our services, we must identify and serve those who face barriers in coming to us.

Whatever your plans for providing outreach service, it is important that you keep the service simple and manageable enough to ensure its continuation. Complicated, costly projects may be doomed to failure once your initial enthusiasm for them is over. It would be unfortunate to begin a service that is highly valued by the recipients and then let it die out because you cannot keep up the momentum. Forget those ideas that take a lot of planning, continued initiative and fancy equipment. Focus instead on such things as group discussions, read-alouds and book delivery. These will be well received and, because the service is simple, it is likely to be long-lived.

TAKING YOUR SERVICES ON THE ROAD

The group most readily identifiable in a community as needing outreach service are those who are home- or institution-bound. Certainly this would include the elderly. Because of physical infirmities or inability to drive, these people are often targeted for library delivery service. Though an obvious group, the elderly are not the only home or institution-bound group. Think about services to daycare centers, to hospitals and to preschools as well.

THE ELDERLY

In serving the elderly who are homebound, you can identify them by a number of methods. First, if you have a meal or home health delivery service in your community, you can use their client list as a place to start. Let the agent who is delivering service to these people know that you are willing to deliver books and ask them to provide you with the names and addresses of their clients who are interested.

Many homebound people, however, do not receive any service from social agencies in your community. They may be cared for at home by family members and thus could be a little harder to identify. Placing public service announcements in the newspapers and on the radio with the library's phone number may encourage those in need of home delivery library service to call. You can also put an article in your library's newsletter letting current patrons know you can provide home delivery service and asking for referrals.

While it may seem like a lot of effort to reach out and serve the homebound elderly in your community, in reality it takes very little. Once you have created a list of patrons who will receive your delivery service (not usually a long list in small communities), you can pick one or two days a month when the service will be provided.

Successful services to the elderly in institutions can include a reading and then discussion of—picture books! Elderly people who have been away from the rites of grandparenting for years now will be thrilled to see what is going on in the picture-book world. We all know that the quality of both text and especially of illustration has become, in many cases, exemplary over the years. Those who haven't had exposure to children's books in recent years will be pleasantly surprised. Then, too, the reading of picture books is much less demanding, making them especially good for groups with diminished attention spans and health.

Who doesn't like to reminisce? The older you become, the more you have to talk about. Try bringing vignettes from local history books and poems by local poets to read aloud and spark discussion of the area's past. These talks are often lively and delightful, and the staff member or volunteer who presents the program will inevitably learn something new about the community's history. If you have a group who is interested in talking about the past, you might persuade someone from the local historical society or a folklore enthusiast to come and talk about the history of your town or state. If during your visits you find that there are other popular interests, address them by getting other local experts to come as guests.

CHILDREN

As fewer and fewer parents are at home during the day, outreach service to day-care providers and preschools is becoming increasingly important. Many of these providers are unable to bring their charges into the library so it's important to bring the library to them. It would be wonderful to have a van or bookmobile complete with a staff member to deliver programs (a grant opportunity perhaps?), but if this isn't possible within your current limitations, you can probably find other effective ways to ensure children in daycare do get library services. Try contacting all the providers you identify and offer them enhanced collections that might include puppets, learning toys, and flannel boards along with the books. You can offer these enhanced collections for extended loan periods and even offer delivery and pick up (this not only adds value to the service but helps to ensure you get materials back). If you develop a number of these special collections, you can rotate them among the providers with relative ease.

SHORT-TERM CARE

Your Friends group might be willing to purchase a special collection of children's paperbacks that your library can give to the local hospital for children who are in their care. Also, consider culling some the best and most interesting books from the book sale to send over to the hospital for their general patients. If the hospital doesn't currently have a structure that would support a small popular library, you might want to talk to them about starting one. Not only will you be providing a wonderful service to people in their time of need, but you will also be promoting your library to nonusers and it's likely they'll become library users when they're able.

The actual delivery of the books or other library material is a perfect job for a volunteer looking for a meaningful way to give their time. Several hours a month may be sufficient to make the rounds, and look what you get in return—you get the satisfaction of knowing that you have brought a welcome diversion and stimulation into what is probably a lonely life. But don't take my word for it; your homebound patrons will sing your praises every delivery day.

People confined to institutional care can offer a chance for greater creativity in delivery of library services. Because you are dealing with a group setting, you can consider not only delivering library materials, but some programming as well. At the expense of just a couple of hours a month, you can enrich your book-delivery service.

KNOWING WHEN TO QUIT

Perhaps nothing is harder than admitting defeat, especially if it involves what you thought was the best idea you ever had. It is important, however, to face the fact when your service to a particular clientele is a waste of time. It happens now and then that no matter what you try, the people you are bringing service to are just not interested. It's time to quit, at least for a while.

As simple as your service might be, it is costing your library. Even if the service is delivered by a volunteer, that volunteer's time is valuable to you. If it becomes evident after an honest effort at engaging the audience that they just aren't responding, make an adjustment. Offer to continue the material delivery service if it is being used, but forget the rest. In the end, outreach, as all services, must be evaluated on the basis of whether or not it is truly filling a need. If you are convinced that the need is genuine, go back to the drawing board and see if there is another more effective way of addressing it. By talking to the volunteer or staff delivering the service as well as the intended recipients, you are likely to find that you can meet special needs in other, more effective ways.

INVISIBLE FUTURE PATRONS

While the home and institution-bound members of your community are obvious targets for outreach, there may be a significant number of people who are much more "invisible." These people may be undereducated, illiterate, culturally different, or simply poor, and thus socially isolated from your public library. The barrier they face (in addition to an inability to read in some cases) is the fear that the unknown can bring.

You should realize that as welcoming, cheery and light as you see your library, there are other people who imagine it to be dark, foreboding, pretentious, unfriendly, and intimidating. People who have no background in library use, who would never imagine libraries to be a part of their world, are isolated by their own assumptions. This is probably the hardest barrier for us to breach and we might only succeed in doing so on a one-to-one basis. If you make contact with the socially and economically disadvantaged members of your community through those already serving their needs, you may find a way to show them that you (and other members of the library staff) are friendly and approachable. If a new library user knows someone to ask for, they may be more likely to come to the library for the first time.

LIBRARIES AND LITERACY

I believe that literacy in this country is a matter of national security. It is that vital to our interests as a leader nation and for the well-being of every citizen. If our citizens cannot read, they cannot compete for jobs—jobs that increasingly require not only a basic level of reading ability but a basic level of computer literacy as well. Nothing threatens our society like poverty and nothing contributes to poverty more than illiteracy. It is estimated that 80 percent of America's prison inmates are functionally illiterate. I don't know how you determine cause and effect in this area, but the sheer numbers certainly do it for me.

Libraries have always played a critical role in helping people successfully live their lives. Since their inception, the public library has been the entity through which people can get the information they need to improve their lot in life. Public libraries are often referred to as the people's university, and it is because of this vital role we play in supporting self-education and self-improvement. Now, as the stakes get raised in the job market, as we see the disappearance of jobs in areas that require manual labor and little to no literacy skills, we are a country at risk if we don't use every tool and institution at hand to fight illiteracy. That includes libraries.

Adults and Literacy

Recently, illiteracy has received heightened recognition as a serious problem in our society. In response to this, literacy groups have sprung up across the country to help address the issue by teaching illiterate adults how to read and by educating the public about the problem. Libraries are in a position to help and they should. If your community has a literacy program, you should contact the people in charge. Let them know that the library is interested in serving the needs of adult new readers and find out how you can best do it.

In addition to offering space for tutors, you can offer to have a staff member meet with the tutor and student on a one-to-one basis to give a tour of the library. Be sure that whoever is representing the library is someone who is friendly and approachable. A new reader is much more likely to come into your library if she has someone to ask for by name.

Your collection, too, should have materials that respond to the special needs of adult new readers. Be sure to include high-interest, low-reading- level materials in your collection. You should not only make these materials available, but let the adult basic education and literacy groups know you have them. Shelve them in a location that makes them readily available to those who are interested.

Making the extra effort to serve those who could as easily go unserved is only doing what we ought to do. We are not heroes for doing our jobs. Nevertheless, there are rewards for service to those in isolation that transcend any paycheck or normal sense of job satisfaction.

One day stands out for me above all others. The service our library provided to a nontraditional user came back in a very unexpected way. I was at the front desk one afternoon, anxiously awaiting the outcome of a hotly contested bond vote for a new addition to our library. My nervous vigilance was interrupted when a middle-aged woman raced in out of breath and clearly jubilant. She wanted to tell me that she voted for the first time in her life because she was finally able to read the ballot. She said she had learned to read at the library, where she and her tutor met every week. She had also attended a reading-discussion group the library sponsored for adult new readers. She was happy to announce that her first vote was a *yes* for the library.

Hearing this proclamation made me know for sure that we would win the vote. I knew it simply because this woman had voted yes. I did not regard her as an omen; rather, I knew that if the library could have this kind of impact on one person's life, we were surely having an impact on the lives of many of the people who used our library. I felt sure these people would support us. And they did!

Children and Literacy

If you can make inroads into reducing illiteracy for adults, imagine the opportunity you have to combat it at its roots. Children who live in homes where reading and books are not valued are not very likely to show up in your children's room. There are children in this country (and your community) who will not have exposure to books until they enter the school system. Children who do not have experience with books prior to school are at a major disadvantage with other children. Clearly, serving these children should be included in a public library's mission.

Children in social or cultural isolation can be identified and served by every library no matter how small. Find out who in your area is providing social service to children and talk to them. As overburdened as social workers already are, I guarantee you they will be happy that you are interested in addressing the special needs of these children.

Social workers in your area can help you determine the best approach. It might be a matter of starting a home delivery program for these children. It might mean that a collection of children's books are shelved at a social agency outlet with very loose circulation rules. You might be able to find a way to provide story hours or other programs for them. If you have the desire, you are likely to find a way.

GROUPS AND ORGANIZATIONS

Not all outreach service, however, is designed to reach those facing barriers. Some is designed to highlight particular collections and services to groups with special interests and needs—even if some members of the group are already using the library. Outreach to groups is a wonderful way to market your wares while increasing your value to different segments of the community. In addition to that, service to groups does not need to be an ongoing enterprise. In many cases a once-a-year visit is all you need to let members of special groups and organizations know how you can serve them.

In planning an outreach program for area organizations, you should determine not only who they are, but what their particular interests are and how the library can respond to them. Groups can include business organizations, the Parent-Teacher Association, schools, health support groups and even your own town council.

Groups organize in the first place because they have a special interest in common and want to share experience and information. The information you have in the library might well be of value to them and they might be unaware of its existence. A sort of "dog and pony show" to the local business association, for example, can be an effective way to show off such resources as the *Value Line, The Wall Street Journal*, your business magazines, your over-the-phone reference service, and your information-rich website.

SCHOOLS

Yearly visits to schools should be a mandatory part of the children's librarian's schedule so that she can introduce herself to the kids and discuss mutual goals with teachers. School visits are invaluable for making the public library's resources known. In addition, you can remind teachers to let you know before sending all the troops in with assignments on the same subject, on which you happen to have exactly three books!

One children's librarian whom I know makes sure that every classroom gets a visit, but she does it by delegating. Everyone from the director to the page gets enlisted and armed with a preselected book to read and with bookmarks for all the children. It's a mutually satisfying experience, and it works.

THE TOWN LEADERS

Finally, while you're out on the road, don't neglect your town government and administration. Pick a time as far away from budget planning as possible and ask to be put on the town council's agenda. Of course, the *real* reason you're going is to show off, brag, and earn a little more respect. All *they* need to know is that you are eager to become better acquainted with their needs for information so that you might be able to serve them better (or serve them at all—we know how often they come in).

Take in your most impressive resources and let them know that they can call with reference questions. If you don't have a laptop and projector, see if you can find one so that you can give the town leaders a cyber-tour through your library's website. This is a good time to throw in a "by the way" such as, "You should never hesitate to call, we really do have a fine reference service. In fact, statistics show that last year we successfully answered more than 500 reference questions over the phone and now we are getting even more through email." When you tell them about your up-to-date business collection, let them know that the response to your collection has been gratifying—circulation rose another 8 percent last year.

While you have the floor, tell them about any special programs coming up and how nice it would be to see them there. It may be hard to believe at times, but your town officials are human. This means among other things that they probably have children or grandchildren. Don't leave out the children's room and all the fine things going on there. Ask them to drop by sometime with the kids to check out some books or attend a children's program.

While you are busy "finding out how you can serve them" let them know how well you are doing. Inform them that you are working with the literacy project, for instance, to encourage library use by adult new readers. Tell them about that elderly woman who is so grateful for home delivery service that she sends you a letter of thanks every year along with a $10 gift. Let them know that more people are using the library than ever before. In short, inform them that their library is a source of pride for the community and that it is the civic center for learning and intellectual stimulation for everyone.

Friends of the Library "Statement of Purpose" (Sample)

The Friends of the Smalltown Public Library work to promote the library within the community and to enhance its resources and services through gifts. The Friends work with the library director and the library trustees in establishing goals for library service.

The Friends of the Smalltown Public Library recognize the value of libraries in our society and the particular value of our own public library in Smalltown. In order to assist the library in preserving and improving its level of service to the people of Smalltown, the Friends will work to provide programs designed to create interest in the library and the issues that face it. In addition, the Friends will act as a political support group when the library's financial resources are being threatened or when the need for additional resources is presented by the library director and the board of trustees.

In order to enhance the level of service currently available, the Friends of Smalltown Public Library will investigate avenues for fundraising which may include, but are not limited to, the sale of gift or withdrawn books and the solicitation of gifts through the Friends newsletter.

All fundraising by the Friends will be in accordance with library policy and all gifts to the library will be made with the approval of the library director.

Orientation Checklist

Welcome to the Smithville Public Library! We believe that our staff is our most valuable asset because we believe excellent public service is not possible without you. In order to help ensure that you have all the information you need to be a success in your new job, we have developed a special orientation program. Within the first two weeks of your employment with us, you'll have an excellent understanding of our values and commitment to service. In addition you'll know what expectations we have of you and your performance. You will learn about the history and current structure of Smithville Public Library. Finally, you'll know such important details as when you'll get paid and what benefits come along with this job!

Enclosed in this orientation packet you'll find the following:
- *Smithville Public Library Mission Statement*
- *Smithville Public Library Statement of Service Philosophy*
- *Position Description*
- *Smithville Public Library Newsletter*
- *Smithville Public Library Organization Chart*
- *Smithville Public Library: a History (pamphlet)*
- *Smithville Public Library Strategic Plan (Executive Summary)*
- *City of Smithville description of employment benefits*

Job Description Worksheet

Worksheet job descriptions should be an honest reflection of the *full scope* of the position. Job worth is often determined by job description. The following is a list of factors often involved in job analyses and evaluations: education, experience, judgment and initiative, supervision required, accountability, contact with others, confidentiality, physical environment, manual skills, physical effort, occupational risks, character of supervision, scope of supervision.

Give the job description serious thought and don't sell yourself or your staff short. Include safety risks, for example (you work in a building that is open to anyone both during the day and at night without security). Include the fact that some jobs require lifting (have you weighed one of those boxes of books lately?). Explain that you work with public confidences. Finally, don't forget such things as stress and the need to think quickly and accurately in handling reference questions.

Now that you have thought seriously about *all* the components of library work, you can begin to put it in writing!

1. Job identification including
   a. Title _____
   b. Under supervision of _____
   c. Supervises _____
   _____
   _____

2. Work to be performed, including
   a. Responsibilities (prioritize) _____
   _____
   b. How duties are performed _____
   _____
   _____
   _____

(Job Description Worksheet, continued)

    c. Why these duties are important to the organization as a whole (include a statement explaining the impact performance has on overall quality of service) ____

_____

_____

_____

3. Knowledge required for position including
   a. Minimum requirements for formal education _____
   b. Minimum years of previous experience _____
   c. Minimum years of specialized experience (define) _____

   _____

   d. Specialized knowledge and expertise _____

   _____

   _____

4. Skills required including
   a. Mental (computational, analytical, abstract) _____

   _____

   b. Technical _____
   c. Physical _____
   d. Interpersonal _____

5. Physical demands including
   a. Exertion _____
   b. Stress _____
   c. Safety _____
   d. Environmental (physical working conditions) _____

   _____

6. Special demands including
   a. Work hours _____
   b. Travel _____
   c. Isolation _____

Personnel Policy Worksheet

Before developing your own personnel policy, you should check with your town's personnel officer to see if the library is covered in the town's own personnel policy. If the library is a town department, you may find you are fully (if not adequately or fairly) covered by the town's policy. If this is the case, you should check it carefully to make sure it applies fairly to you and your staff (e.g., you work Saturdays and evenings—do other town employees?). In addition, you can make any needed improvements by campaigning with the town's administration to be actively involved in the policy's update when the time comes.

Even if you are not covered by the town's policy (your direct governance by a Board of Trustees might well exempt you), there may be some broad constraints included in town government within which you must operate. Be sure you are aware of any rules or laws which will apply to you and your staff and incorporate them in the policy.

Once you are familiar with what is expected of you by the town, you can begin to work with your staff and the Board of Trustees to design a document that best suits your own particular circumstances.

The Personnel Policy should include the following:

1. Statement declaring the value of library personnel and an adherence to a practice of non-discrimination: _____
_____
_____
_____

2. Definition of types of employees, including:
   a. Full-time (how many hours per week) _____
   b. Part-time (what aspects of the policy are they exempt from) _____
   _____
   _____
   _____

(Personnel Policy Worksheet, continued)

   c. Temporary (define conditions of this type of employment) _____
_____
_____

3. Benefits including:
   a. Vacation time (how much, how frequent, how administered) _____
_____
_____

   b. Sick leave (how accumulated and at what rate) _____
_____

   c. Other paid time off (including caring for sick family members, funeral leave, jury duty, personal time, paid holidays, maternity/ paternity leave) _____
_____
_____

   d. Scholarships and paid association dues _____
_____

   e. Health care (including medical, dental, mental, eye) _____
_____
_____

   f. Retirement benefits (how administered and how paid) _____
_____
_____

   g. Disability and life insurance (how it is administered and under what circumstances) _____
_____
_____

4. Termination including:
   a. Notice required of full-time employees _____
   b. Notice required of part-time employees _____
   c. Procedure for terminating employees (include number of written warnings which will be given and what would provoke immediate dismissal) _____
_____
_____

5. Grievance procedure including:
   a. How employee officially protests a poor performance review _____
_____
_____

   b. How to appeal to trustees for re-evaluation _____
_____
_____

Sample Volunteer Job Description

Library Materials Processor

The library materials processor covers and prepares library materials to make them more attractive and to increase their durability before they are made available to the public.

DUTIES AND RESPONSIBILITIES

- Covers books, both hardcover and paperback, in accordance with established library procedure (for specific instructions, see instruction sheets for individual library materials).
- Processes videos, cassettes, CDs, and other library media in accordance with established library procedure (for specific instructions, see instruction sheets for individual library media).
- Follows inventory procedures for processing supplies and notifies supervisor when replacements need to be ordered.
- Repairs and replaces worn or damaged book covers as necessary and informs supervisor when repair or replacement of covers is not possible or attractive.
- Recommends new procedures or supplies that might make the processing of materials easier, less expensive, more enduring and/or more attractive.

POSITION REQUIREMENTS

This position requires good handiwork skills, along with neatness and attention to detail. The person in this position should be able to follow simple inventory procedures and be able to judge when the condition of book and media covers will make the materials unsuitable for patron use.

Volunteer Application Form

NAME _____

PHONE _____

ADDRESS _____

CONTACT PERSON (in case of emergency) _____

_____   Phone _____

1. List past work experience (including volunteer work). Highlight the experience which you feel might be applicable to library work.

2. List other skills and special knowledge you have which might be beneficial to the library.

3. Why are you interested in working at Smalltown Library?

4. Are you interested in all aspects of library work? Are there some jobs you are not interested in?

5. Would you prefer to have a regular work schedule or work on special projects within a more flexible time frame?

6. Are there any days or times of day when you are not available?

7. How many hours per week/month would you have to give to the library?

REFERENCES:

1. _____

   _____ Phone _____

2. _____

   _____ Phone _____

Volunteers at Smalltown Library are as important to its function as any other members of the staff. Because we rely on our volunteers to enable us to provide the best service possible to the community, we ask that they commit to an agreed-upon schedule and give reasonable notice if they are unable to report to work. Excessive absences make it difficult for us to work efficiently. If a volunteer finds that he or she must miss work frequently, the library may find it necessary to replace him or her with someone who is able to be on hand on a regular basis.

Volunteers are required to attend staff meetings one to three times per year. Each volunteer will be evaluated individually on a formal basis once a year and informally on a regular basis.

The librarian will determine the nature and scope of each volunteer's job in the library after the initial interview.

I have read the above and understand my responsibilities as a volunteer at Smalltown Library.

Signed _____

Date _____

Library Bill of Rights

The American Library Association affirms that all libraries are forums for information and ideas, and that the following basic policies should guide their services.

I. Books and other library resources should be provided for the interest, information, and enlightenment of all people of the community the library serves. Materials should not be excluded because of the origin, background, or views of those contributing to their creation.

II. Libraries should provide materials and information presenting all points of view on current and historical issues. Materials should not be proscribed or removed because of partisan or doctrinal disapproval.

III. Libraries should challenge censorship in the fulfillment of their responsibility to provide information and enlightenment.

IV. Libraries should cooperate with all persons and groups concerned with resisting abridgment of free expression and free access to idea.

V. A person's right to use a library should not be denied or abridged because of origin, age, background, or views.

VI. Libraries which make exhibit spaces and meeting rooms available to the public they serve should make such facilities available on an equitable basis, regardless of the beliefs or affiliations of individuals or groups requesting their use.

Adopted June 18, 1948.
Amended February 2, 1961, and January 23, 1980;
inclusion of "age" in v. reaffirmed January 23, 1996,
by the ALA Council.

American Library Association Code of Ethics

As members of the American Library Association, we recognize the importance of codifying and making known to the profession and to the general public the ethical principles that guide the work of librarians, other professionals providing information services, library trustees and library staffs.

Ethical dilemmas occur when values are in conflict. The American Library Association Code of Ethics states the values to which we are committed, and embodies the ethical responsibilities of the profession in this changing information environment.

We significantly influence or control the selection, organization, preservation, and dissemination of information. In a political system grounded in an informed citizenry we are members of the profession in this changing information environment.

We significantly influence or control the selection, organization, preservation, and dissemination of information. In a political system grounded in an informed citizenry we are members of a profession explicitly committed to intellectual freedom and the freedom of access to information. We have a special obligation to ensure the free flow of information and ideas to resent and future generations.

The principles of this Code are expressed in broad statements to guide ethical decision making. These statements provide a framework; they cannot and do not dictate conduct to cover particular situations.

I.   We provide the highest level of service to all library users through appropriate and usefully organized resources; equitable service policies; equitable access; and accurate, unbiased, and courteous responses to all requests.

II. We uphold the principles of intellectual freedom and resist all efforts to censor library resources.

III. We protect each library user's right to privacy and confidentiality with respect to information sought or received and resources consulted, borrowed, acquired or transmitted.

IV. We recognize and respect intellectual property rights.

V. We treat co-workers and other colleagues with respect, fairness and good faith, and advocate conditions of employment that safeguard the rights and welfare of all employees of our institutions.

VI. We do not advance private interests at the expense of library users, colleagues, or our employing institutions.

VII. We distinguish between our personal convictions and professional duties and do not allow our personal beliefs to interfere with fair representation of the aims of our institutions or the provision of access to their information resources.

VIII. We strive for excellence in the profession by maintaining and enhancing our own knowledge and skills, by encouraging the professional development of co-workers, and by fostering the aspirations of potential members of the profession.

Adopted by the ALA Council
June 28, 1995

Yourtown Public Library Internet Use Policy

The Yourtown Public Library (YPL) provides computing resources which allow public access to a variety of networked electronic resources, including in-house databases, the Internet, and U.S. government publications in electronic format, and to YPL-owned software such as word-processing and publishing programs. YPL reserves the right to set rules as needed to promote equitable computer use and to revise this policy in response to changes in, or concerns about, YPL's computing environment.

USER RESPONSIBILITIES

Users are responsible for the following to ensure fair and proper use of library computing resources.

Conduct: Users must observe the Library Code of Conduct as it specifically relates to use of the library computer resources.

Copyright: Users must observe copyright and communication laws.

Equipment: Users may not tamper with or reconfigure equipment, software, or data belonging to the library or other users.

Prohibitions: Library employees and patrons may not use the library's computer equipment for sending, receiving, viewing, or downloading illegal material via the Internet.

Privacy: Users must observe the right of others to privacy.

Software: Use of nonlibrary software is not permitted.

Sounds and visuals: Users shall refrain from the use of sounds and visuals which disrupt the ability of other library patrons or the staff to use the library and its resources.

(Yourtown Public Library Internet Use Policy, continued)

INTERNET-SPECIFIC USER RESPONSIBILITIES

A global network of computers, the Internet provides access to a wide variety of education, recreational, and reference resources, many of which are not available in print, but there is no central control over its content or users. Library patrons use the Internet at their own discretion. The library does not protect persons from information found individually offensive. Due to the nature of the Internet, YPL staff may be limited in their ability to provide assistance.

Children and the Internet: It is the responsibility of the parents and the guardians of minor children to supervise the access and use of the Internet in the Library by their children. Parental consent for a library card constitutes acknowledgment by that parent that they have responsibility for monitoring their child's use of all library resources. Library employees will casually monitor children's Internet use to assist and guide them.

Evaluation: YPL cannot ensure the availability or the accuracy of external electronic resources. Like print materials, not all electronic materials provide accurate, complete, or current information. Users need to be good information consumers, questioning the validity of information.

SANCTIONS

Libraries rely upon the cooperation of their users in order to efficiently and effectively provide shared resources and ensure community access to a wide range of information. If individuals break these acceptable use rules in any way, their right to networked resources may be suspended for a specified time, depending on the damage caused by their actions. Individuals using library computing resources for illegal purposes may also be subject to prosecution.

Adopted by YPL Board of Trustees, March 1, 2002

Request for Reconsideration of Library Material

Name of individual initiating request _____

Address _____

City _____ State ____ Zip _____ Telephone _____

Author/Producer of Work _____

Format: Book ____ Video ____ Spoken Word ____ CD ____ Other _____

1. What exactly do you object to in this material? (Please be specific; i.e., cite pages where possible. Use back of form if necessary.) _____

_____

_____

_____

2. For what age group would you recommend this material? _____

3. Did you read or view the entire work? _____ If not, what parts did you read or view? _____

4. In your opinion, is there anything of value in this material? _____

_____

_____

5. Is there another title you would recommend in place of this one? _____

_____

6. Do you have any additional comments you would like to make about this material? _____

Date _____ Signature _____

Thank you for your comments. This request will be reviewed by the Library's Selection Review Committee. You should receive a response in four weeks.

Gift Acknowledgment/ Receipt (Sample)

Thank you for your generous gift.

Anytown Public Library will accept your **NEW** and **USED**:

- Books
- Videos
- Audiocassettes (Books-on-tape)
- Music (CDs only)

We cannot accept damaged materials, most magazines, condensed books, software, most textbooks, and music other than compact discs. Please call 555-READ for more information. Thank you for your support.

Donations may be delivered to the library Monday–Friday from 10:00 A.M. to 5:00 P.M.

The library will determine if donated items meet material selection guidelines. Items not selected may be placed in the Friends of the Library book sale.

For Your Records:

_____ books, videos, audiocassettes, and/or _____ were received from _____ *(giver)* on _____ *(date)*.

Anytown Public Library

Meeting Room Policy (Sample)

The meeting room of the Smalltown Public Library is an important component of the library's services. It is available to any community group, regardless of that group's political, religious or social views, during hours when the library is open or closed, subject to the following:

1. All meetings must be scheduled in advance with the library. Library programs will have precedence for use of the meeting room. No group may schedule meetings for more than one year in advance or for more than one use per month (special exceptions may be made by the librarian).

2. All meetings must be open to the public.

3. No person or group may charge an attendance fee for meetings or workshops held in the meeting room or make requests for voluntary donations. Charges to cover costs of materials *may* be levied if the person or group has the express written permission of the librarian in advance.

4. The building is to be kept locked at all times when the library is closed. There fore, when a group is using the meeting room while the rest of the library is closed, the person signing this agreement will be held responsible for:
   a. getting a key for the exterior entrance not more than 24 hours prior to the meeting;
   b. returning the key in the bookdrop of the library immediately following the meeting; and
   c. making sure all doors and windows are securely shut and locked in the meeting room upon leaving.

THE GROUP USING THE MEETING ROOM WILL BE HELD RESPONSIBLE FOR ANY AND ALL LOSSES INCURRED BY THE LIBRARY AS A RESULT OF LEAVING THE BUILDING UNLOCKED.

(Meeting Room Policy, continued)

5. The meeting room must be left in the same condition in which it was found. Any tables or chairs rearranged should be returned to their original places. If the kitchen was used, it must be cleaned and all utensils, appliances, or dishes used must be washed and put away.

THERE WILL BE A MINIMUM CHARGE OF $10.00 IF THE MEETING ROOM OR KITCHEN IS NOT LEFT IN ITS ORIGINAL CONDITION.

6. No smoking is allowed in any part of the library at any time.

The signing of this policy constitutes an agreement by the undersigned to adhere to the rules of the Meeting Room Policy and to ensure that no member of the group violates the rules set forth.

Signed _____   Date _____

For _____
                            (Group Name)

Building Program—
Facility Checklist (Sample)

Before the architect comes up with even rudimentary design proposals, he or she will need to understand how the building should work. The checklist below can function as a worksheet for you, your staff, and the architect or building consultant to identify what kinds of needs you'll have in each discrete space in your new or expanded library. What services need to be colocated or in close proximity to one another? What services should be kept separate (childen's room from quiet study, for example). This checklist will also spell out in clear detail what types of furniture you'll need and how the room will be used. Your architect or building consultant will be able to help you translate your projected use into square footage and eventually into an ideal layout.

Name of Space: _____

Floor Area: _____

Users: _____

Purpose: _____

Breakdown of Space: _____

Physical Relationship to Other Space: _____

Special Requirements: _____

    Lighting: _____

    Electrical: _____

    Computing (including wiring and telecommunications requirements): _____

    _____

    Acoustical: _____

    Phone: _____

(Building Program—Facility Checklist, continued)

Plumbing: _____

Heat/vent/AC: _____

Other (floor covering, etc.): _____

Fixed Furniture and Equipment: _____

Movable Furniture and Equipment: _____

Annotated Bibliography

CHAPTER ONE.
CREATING A POLITICAL BASE

Dolnick, Sandy [editor]. *Friends of Libraries,* 3rd edition. Chicago: American Library Association, 1996. 313 pages, index.

You gotta have Friends and this is the book to help you either develop a new Friends group or work more effectively with the group you have. In addition to the nuts and bolts of Friends development, this book—a collection of essays by leaders in our field—discusses Friends and their role in library advocacy. Also helpful for you and your Friends is good solid practical advice in raising money, setting up a gift shop, growing the membership and planning events. Sample bylaws and checklists for the development of various programs and strategies are included.

Gorman, Michael. *Our Singular Strengths: Meditations for Librarians.* Chicago: American Library Association, 1998. 196 pages.

This lovely book should be required reading for all librarians. Exploring and celebrating our very reason for being, this collection of meditations will provoke thought and also pride in what we have dedicated our lives to doing. On "Small Libraries are Beautiful," Gorman says, "Though huge libraries can inspire awe, it is very often the small library that inspires affection." At the end of this meditation, he says, "I will maintain the humanity of small libraries in libraries large and small."

Our professional values, conflicts, and services are all explored and considered. Keep a copy of this book on your desk and retreat to it from time to time to restore your librarian soul.

Reed, Sally Gardner. *Making the Case for Your Library.* New York: Neal-Schuman Publishers, Inc., 2001. 143 pages. Appendix. Index.

A how-to-do-it manual that will provide you with all the information you need to develop an ongoing campaign of support for your library and how to wage a campaign for a specific cause such as a bond issue or an increase in your operating budget. We are beginning to understand that we must move beyond simple "marketing" of our services to showing our decision-makers why what we do matters. In addition, we have to learn how to make the case for library funding in a time when the future of libraries is being questioned by civic leaders. This book will show you how, with samples and illustrations from libraries across the country that are already doing it right.

Reed, Sally Gardner. *Saving Your Library: Getting, Using and Keeping the Power You Need!* Jefferson, NC: McFarland & Company, Inc., 1992. 133 pages. Index.

The concerned librarian needs practical, useful advice for snaring financial support—and this book abounds with ideas on the subject. Part One looks at library advocacy on the local level from immediate concerns to ongoing support strategies. Part Two examines tactics to garner state and federal support. No one knows better than librarians the benefits libraries provide or the perils they face, so no one is more qualified to be the voice to save libraries.

Ross, Catherine Sheldrick, and Patricia Dewdney. *Communicating Professionally: A How-to-Do-It-Manual for Library Applications,* 2nd edition. New York: Neal-Schuman, 1998. [How-to-do-it manual—series edited by Bill Katz.] 293 pages. Index. Bibliography.

An important component to being an effective advocate for your library is your ability to communicate effectively. This book will help even the novice communicator come across as polished and effective. In addition to focusing on public speaking—the obvious communication tool—this book addresses the importance of active listening, effective one-on-one communication (often the most difficult), writing, and even body language. *Communicating Professionally* also presents strategies for working effectively in groups and being seen as a leader in them—an important skill because you'll want to be seen as both a team player and a leader by your town government in your involvement with community organizations. Finally, because you can't make your library's case by yourself, the book concludes with a chapter on how to train others on staff and among your supporters to become effective communicators as well.

Young, Virginia G. *The Library Trustee: A Practical Guidebook,* 5th edtion. Chicago: American Library Association, 1995. 251 pages. Index.

In addition to helping you develop (and stand behind) library policy, your trustees can and should be your front line in promoting libraries and their services. The trustees can make the case for funding and work hard to promote the library's budget. Virginia Young is *the* reigning expert in developing and maximizing your trustees. This outlines the roles and responsibilities of trustees, discusses ways in which trustees can keep abreast of the important issues facing libraries, how trustees can work effectively and well with staff, and trustees in the future of the library. Also included in this book are samples of such things as policies, by-laws, budgets, and ethics statements.

CHAPTER TWO.
PERSONNEL—THE LIBRARY'S MOST VALUABLE ASSET

Belcastro, Patricia. *Evaluating Library Staff: A Performance Appraisal System.* Chicago: American Library Association, 1998. 253 pages. Index.

It is not enough to hire and train employees; it is also important that library employees get feedback and good critical support for growing and getting better in their jobs. This easy-to-use book will help any library director develop and implement a good and effective evaluation strategy. Included is information on developing performance standards, coaching the employee, documenting behavior and substandard performance, and giving employees a good and fair evaluation. This book includes case studies and sample documents. Evaluations often get ignored by library directors, or they are seen as a burden and waste of time. Ask any employee, and you'll find they're not. This book will get you on track and help you be a better coach and leader.

Bessler, Joanne M. *Putting Service Into Library Staff Training: A Library Manager's Training Guide.* Chicago: American Library Association, 1994. 72 pages. Index.

A quick read, this book gets to the heart of the matter. Service is what we are all about and, therefore, service should be at the heart of our staff development efforts. This little book examines recruitment, orientation, defining your library's service goals and empowering your staff to carry them out. Included is a training module for effective telephone service, along with special instruction and advice in handling an angry patron, and selling the library's services.

Lewis, Audrey. *Madame Audrey's Guide to Mostly Cheap But Good Reference Books for Small and Rural Libraries*. Chicago: American Library Association, 1998. 206 pages. Index.

The title just about says it all! Audrey, herself a director of a small library, provides a good list of basic resources that every small library should have. Arranged by categories that reflect those of the Dewey Decimal System, affordable reference works are listed and evaluated. A handy, easy to use guide, that hopefully will be updated every couple of years.

Lipow, Anne Grodzins, and Deborah A. Carvers (editors). *Staff Development: A Practical Guide*, 2nd edition. Chicago: American Library Association, 1992.

Going beyond just the how to, this book begins with a good look at how people learn. This foundational underpinning is important for the development of effective strategies and programs to help train staff. This collection of essays includes information on how to plan for development, how to implement effective programs, and most importantly, how to make sure that "training sticks." Various statements on the importance and definition of staff development are appended as are suggestions for further reading.

McDaniel, Julie Ann, and Judith K. Ohles. *Training Paraprofessionals for Reference Service: A How-to-Do-It Manual for Librarians*. New York: Neal-Schman, 1993. 180 pages. Index.

In all likelihood, your library will not have a separate full-time reference librarian—or if it does, it is just as likely that many of your patrons' questions will be answered by a paraprofessional on duty. This book is here to help. Included is information on how to evaluate the level of training needed, orienting paraprofessionals to reference service, and training modules. In addition, you will find lists of typical types of reference questions along with strategies for answering them effectively. While this book tends to have a bit of an academic bent, the techniques for training and evaluation can easily be transferred to the public library environment.

Reed, Sally Gardner. *Library Volunteers: Worth the Effort!* Jefferson, NC: McFarland & Company, Inc., 1992. 122 pages. Index.

Volunteers are critical to the success of any small libraries. Not only do we need them for the tremendous assistance they can provide, but volunteers can also be our best spokespeople in the community—they are always out there making the case for the importance of libraries and the importance of funding libraries. This book will help you set up and manage an excellent volunteer force. It includes advice on how to manage difficult volunteers, how to recruit and train, and how to show your appreciation. Also included are sample volunteer job descriptions, training worksheets, thank you certificates, and more.

Trotta, Marcia. *Successful Staff Development: A How-to-Do-It Manual*. New York: Neal-Schuman, 1995. 112 pages.

This book starts out with "What They Didn't Teach You in Library School," so right away you know it's going to be good. From there, Trotta goes on to define staff development, discuss staff development programs, and show how to maximize the individual strengths on your staff. Included are actual programs, curricula, and handouts. The second half of the book presents methods on effective evaluation and staff recognition. Keeping your staff well trained and motivated is absolutely essential to their ability to deliver excellent services—this book will help you do your job in keeping staff able to do theirs.

CHAPTER THREE.
THE LIBRARY'S COLLECTION

Gregory, Vicki L. *Selecting and Managing Electronic Resources: A How-to-Do-It-Manual.* New York: Neal-Schuman Publishers, 2000. 109 pages. Index.

What a wonderful time for small libraries. No longer constrained by physical space, small libraries can now offer their patrons the limitless resources available on the web. For many of us, however, this definitely comes under the heading of "What we didn't learn in library school!" Don't worry, this book will help. Though the Internet is changing and growing everyday—adding resources and bells and whistles—Gregory focuses on strategies for good decision-making in integrating electronic resources into your library's more traditional collections. In addition to providing policies and guidelines, she also gives good criteria for and information on budgeting for electronic resources. Helpful worksheets are also included to give even the most "clueless" among us the guidance we need to make smart choices for our electronic collections.

Slote, Stanley J. *Weeding Library Collections: Library Weeding Methods,* 4th edition. Englewood, Colorado, 1997. 240 pages. Index.

I believe that weeding a collection well is the most challenging and important component of collection development. Once you've taken a book off the shelf and relegated it to the booksale (or dumpster), there is usually no going back. Books go out of print quickly and a mistake in weeding may well be irreversible. Luckily, however, there is help in how to do it right. Slote, a frequent writer on this topic, discusses reasons for keeping a well-weeded collection, guidelines to use for weeding, practical advice on how to do it, and how to use technology to help make the job easier. A very comprehensive guide for a very important project.

Smith, Mark. *Internet Policy Handbook for Libraries.* New York: Neal-Schuman Publishers, 1999. 219 pages. Index.

There's no doubt that the Internet has become part of most libraries' collections. This book will help you develop policies and practices that will assist you in managing this resource effectively. Discussed are the principles behind policymaking—how the Internet will reflect and work in concert with your library's mission. Also included are discussions on who should be involved in the policymaking for Internet use. Nuts and bolts of creating a good physical environment are included as is information on developing a comprehensive infrastructure for technology. Finally, the book includes much to think about when considering filters—how, when and if they make sense for your library.

Symons, Ann K., and Sally Gardner Reed (editors). *Speaking Out! Voices in Celebration of Intellectual Freedom.* Chicago: American Library Association, 1999. Indexes.

As we keep up the good fight to ensure that our collections and services remain open to the broadest audiences and free from censorship, it is important and good to know that intellectual freedom has a longstanding place of importance in our democracy and that there are many inside and outside the profession who honor our defense of this principle. This collection of essays is based on famous quotes regarding intellectual freedom, and the contributing writers include actor Edward Asner, Congressman Barney Frank, and author Nat Hentoff. Librarian contributors include such notables as James Billington, Lillian Gerhardt, and Herbert White.

Wynar, Bohdan S. (editor). *Recommended Reference Books for Small and Medium-sized Libraries and Media Centers.* Englewood, Colorado, annual.

This work which comes out each year consists of book reviews chosen from the current edition of the *American Reference Books Annual* and includes dictionaries, encyclopedias, bibliographies and other ready reference types of materials. Organized in broad categories such as "Humanities," "General Reference Works," and "Social Sciences," for example, this evaluative guide gives descriptions, costs, and publishing information on a wide variety of current resources.

CHAPTER FOUR.
THE LIBRARY BUILDING

Brawner, Lee B., and Donald K. Beck, Jr. *Determining Your Public Library's Future Size: A Needs Assessment and Planning Model.* Chicago: American Library Association, 1996. 155 pages. Index.

If you are out of space or not maximizing your existing space well, this book is for you. Divided into three parts, the first part will guide you through a process to determine your space needs. Included in Part I is advice on selecting a consultant and understanding the consultant's role in this process, as well as considerations to make regarding alternatives to construction. Part II is focused on assessing your library's current effectiveness and includes issues such as volunteer support, staffing, finances, and resources. Part III will help you document your present and future space needs, assess the quality and effectiveness of your building, and evaluate alternatives for the future. Helpful appendices include space-planning guidelines, the ins and outs of a building program, and tips on selecting a good building site.

Cirillo, Susan E., and Robert E. Danford. *Library Buildings, Equipment, and the ADA: Compliance Issues and Solutions.* Chicago: American Library Association, 1996. 96 pages. Index.

We librarians talk about access a lot. Usually we are talking about intellectual access; sometimes we are talking about hours of operation; and sometimes we are talking about "virtual" access. Too seldom, we keep the "invisible" minority foremost in our deliberations over access.

If our libraries are not accessible to those with disabilities, we may never see these folks come through our doors—this makes it all too easy to forget about their needs, and the cycle of noncompliance with the Americans with Disabilities Act (ADA) continues. Though there are federal and state mandates for meeting ADA requirements, there is much more we can do than basic compliance—we can make our libraries and our resources truly accessible. This book will help. Beginning with a summary of the ADA, the book moves forward to cover issues of space layout and design, accessible seating, adaptive technologies, and safety and security considerations. You are sure to be introduced to barriers you never even thought about.

Staff of the Williamsburg Regional Library. *Library Construction from a Staff Perspective.* Jefferson, NC: McFarland and Company, Inc., 2001. 170 pages. Index.

All from the perspective of those who work in the library, this book covers the planning process for building or renovating library space, the actual building process, and most importantly, living with the results. Here you will learn how to work effectively with library consultants and architects, how to determine and implement technology upgrades, and how to plan exciting opening-day events. The book includes photographs of building in progress along with a variety of helpful appendices to make the building process go more smoothly. Take it from those who know!

Wells, Marianna, and Rosemary Young. *Moving and Reorganizing a Library.* Hampshire, England: Gower, 1997. 123 pages. Index.

Here's a book that addresses a very important but often underlooked component of a library renovation or building project. Everything is covered from planning a move, to recruiting temporary help, training staff, calculating collection size, preparing the new site, and organizing and making the move. There is excellent advice and instruction on shifting collections for space reasons, determing what's needed to switch to new formats, and deciding on space requirements and layout for furniture. This book will be your best friend as you undertake that (for many of us) once in a life time move to new or newly renovated quarters.

CHAPTER FIVE. SERVICE

Hernon, Peter, and Ellen Altman. *Assessing Service Quality: Satisfying the Expectations of Library Customers*. Chicago: American Library Association, 1998. 243 pages. Index.

In determing where it is you want to go with excellent services, it makes sense to understand where you are. This book will help you do both. It is designed to help you think in new ways about services as you implement them in a changing environment. It will provide guidance in ensuring that service creation includes patron and community input through such methods as focus groups and surveys, and it will help you to effect the changes and improvements in service that you design. Always customer focused, this book will get you moving through the process of assessment, design and implementation of services that best meet the needs of your community.

Larson, Jeanette, and Herman L. Totten. *Model Policies for Small and Medium Public Libraries*. New York: Neal-Schuman, 1998. 212 pages. Index.

Good service begins with good policy. Nothing will help guide your practice better than excellent policy. Not only are policies guidelines, but the very development of policies can help you and your staff re-examine your principles and rethink the ways in which you deliver services. This book provides background and foundation for various types of policies and concludes each discussion with a sample policy. Giving lots of food for thought, it covers such policy areas as staff conduct, use of materials, patron conduct, and access to and use of the facility. Though each library's policies will be unique to the needs of the community it serves, there is much to share and learn from others and this book covers their views and experiences comprehensively.

Miller, Glenn. *Customer Service & Innovation in Libraries*. Ft. Atkinson, Wisconsin: Highsmith Press, 1996. 93 pages. Index.

This is a down-to-earth, practical guide in developing and implementing good service in libraries. From storytelling to "kidsmail," from reference service to a library greeter, this guidebook will answer many questions you've had about initiating or enhancing various types of service, and probably introduce you to some new ideas as well. Going beyond in-house services, this book also discusses books by mail and drive-up windows.

Nelson, Sandra (for the Public Library Association). *The New Planning for Results: A Streamlined Approach*. Chicago: American Library Association, 2001. 315 pages. Index.

Here it is, your new planning bible. This book will give you all the information and guidance you need to plan for your library's future. It is seldom that excellence just happens—it is planned for and designed based on what is happening in your community, what is happening in the library and information world, and what your patrons want from their library. This book understands that our world is changing around us and that excellence is "a moving target." With that in mind, it will help you determine where you are, where you want to go, and how you will know when you get there. It includes suggestions on bringing your community into the planning process and provides you with details of specific planning strategies such as SWOT (strengths, weaknesses, opportunities, threats). Complete with worksheets and samples, this book will take you, your library and your community from vision to implementation effectively.

PLA Policy Manual Committee. *PLA Handbook for Writers of Public Library Policies*. Chicago: Public Library Association (division of the American Library Association), 1993. 72 pages.

Straight to the point, this book provides the framework for the development of practical policies on such matters as interlibrary loan, materials selection, meeting-room use, exhibits, and patron conduct. Sample policies are included. This small, almost pamphletlike guidebook does not include an index and really doesn't need one. A quick glance at the table of contents will send you to the page or pages for the development of the policy you're interested in.

Weingand, Darlene E. *Customer Service Excellence: A Concise Guide for Librarians*. Chicago: American Library Association, 1997. 136 pages. Index.

Weingand has written much on the art and science of library management and this book is a reflection of her commitment to excellence in library services. Easy and quick to read, this book espouses, and encourages the reader to develop, a philosophy of service that underpins all that the library offers. It includes discussions on defining excellence and keeping the customers involved, and strategies for staff development in service delivery and for evaluation of services. Chapters on effective communication, serving a diverse clientele, and developing strong partnerships with your constituencies are also included.